GIFTS FROM THE HOME

A Creative Book of Ideas for Giving

For Casper, Hannes, Herman and Jané

GIFTS FROM THE HOME

A Creative Book of Ideas for Giving

Anika Pretorius

Illustrations by Jacques le Roux and Nicci Page
Photography by James Garaghty

NH
NEW HOLLAND

NEW HOLLAND

First published in the UK in 1989 by
New Holland (Publishers) Ltd
37 Connaught Street
London W2 2AZ

First published 1988

Editor Jan Schaafsma
Design Janice Evans

Typesetting by Diatype Setting cc
Reproduction by Photo Sepro Ltd
Printed by Kyodo Printing Co (S'pore) Pte Ltd

ISBN 1 85368 081 8

Contents

Acknowledgements

When one has compiled a book such as this, thanks are due to so many people.

At the top of the list is Pieter Struik, whose idea it was in the first place. Thanks to his unremitting interest and encouragement, this opportunity he gave me became a wonderfully enriching experience. Jan Schaafsma's friendliness, helpfulness and competent direction meant a lot to me. Janice Evans deserves special mention, because it is she who made this beautiful book out of a dull manuscript. James Garaghty displayed the greatest patience while taking the photographs, and it was a wonderful experience to spend a week working with him, Ingrid Jenkins, who helped with the styling, and Cathy Brophy. Jacques le Roux produced all the explanatory illustrations and cross stitch patterns – an enormous task which he took upon himself with a smile and much enthusiasm. Nicci Page drew and painted the lovely page borders.

I will also never forget the unselfish enthusiasm of all those people whose ideas I was able to use and who helped me to make the samples. The following come to mind: Beverley Pochop who kindly agreed that I could use her original ideas for the wreath and hat decorated with flowers, the posy of dried flowers and the painted gifts. She also made all these samples. Then there's Dana Dean who agreed that I could use and adapt her original idea for the kitchen witch; Anneli Breedt who designed and made the appliqué items; Olga Kersten, always bubbling with enthusiasm, who gave me the go-ahead to use her potpourri recipe; my friend Betsie Lessing who has over the years provided me with numerous original ideas to put into practice; and last, but not least, my mother, who did the beautiful embroidery on the little Hummel characters. I'm so pleased she also made something for the book as it was, after all, she and my grandmother who taught me to make things with my hands. They also made, by hand, most of the decorative cloths used as background in many of the photographs.

Then I'd like to thank the companies that gave me permission to use their designs or patterns: DMC for the cross-stitch design for the kitchen chefs, Paragon Needlecraft and Josef Mueller for the cross-stitch design for the 'Singing Quartet', Burda for the wedding hanger, and Craftways Corporation for 'Home Sweet Home', based on a project which was published in the magazine *Cross Stitch & Country Crafts*.

Many thanks also to Beverley Wagenaar who typed the manuscript and my friend Karin Verreynne who proofread and corrected it.

Finally, there's my own family; thank you for all the assistance, patience and support. The book was actually a team effort. My husband Casper made all the wooden samples and had to help me think when I battled to explain something clearly. He also did all the illustrations for the manuscript. Even our two sons, Hannes and Herman, were always on the lookout for ideas for the book. Jané, our boisterous two-year old daughter, also lent a hand as she sat perched on a chair or on top of the table.

Our cleaning lady, Nelly Skhosana, was often the first to see the completed items and her enthusiastic admiration was a real source of inspiration. And if she hadn't taken on the household chores, I would not have been able to complete this book.

Anika Pretorius 1988

Introduction

A gift you've made yourself has a certain value that money can't buy. In making a gift you're actually giving something of yourself. I truly believe that there's more pleasure in the giving than in the receiving of a gift. After all, it's such fun to make something with loving care and then to see how much someone else appreciates and enjoys it.

The purpose of this book is to provide you with ideas and instructions to make gifts yourself. However, I hope that it will also serve as an inspiration for you to develop any as yet undiscovered sense of creativity. Those who do not use their hands to make things are missing out on so much in life. It's a most rewarding and enriching pastime that has a calming effect and even lets one forget one's aches and pains.

The methods followed in the book are not always strictly according to the rules. Instead, I've tried to give easy, practical methods and hints. I trust that it won't even be necessary to make any trial attempts and that your first effort will be a success.

I hope everyone who makes any of the items in this book, whether as a gift or to keep, will have as much fun as I did in compiling it.

Both metric and imperial measurements are given, but it is a good idea to stick to one system or the other with each gift.

CHAPTER I
Gifts from the kitchen

*I can hardly imagine a book on gifts from the home
that does not include gifts made in the kitchen:
there's always someone who will welcome a delicious
treat. Just think of the friends who seem to have
everything or the neighbours to whom you'd like to
give something their whole family will enjoy.
Mothers with newborn babies will really appreciate,
along with a gift for the new baby, something for
the rest of the family to nibble.
When someone is ill, a gift from the kitchen is a
wonderful way of expressing your concern.
It's also a quick way of making a number of gifts in
one go. You could make sufficient rusks or fudge in
one morning to be gift-wrapped into attractive and
welcome gifts for each of the children's teachers.*

9

Delicious fudge

This is a tasty treat both to give and receive. I've yet to come across someone who does not like fudge. Unfortunately, making fudge can be quite tricky. This recipe, however, is guaranteed to be a success if you follow the instructions precisely.

There's a story to this recipe. For years a certain Mrs Wilson used to make it every week and then sell it at a charity shop. One day she showed me how to make it, and subsequently I've made it time and again for charity sales, fairs, bazaars, birthdays and as Christmas gifts, and I have yet to make a batch that's a failure.

The secret to success is the saucepan. Use a very heavy iron or aluminium saucepan with a heavy base and at least a 5-litre capacity. The pressure cookers of yesteryear (the ones that often went shooting through the ceiling) are ideal. If you are able to lay your hands on one of them, don't let it go! No matter if it's minus the lid, as you won't be needing this.

Fudge should never be hurried either. If it boils too rapidly, it will stick to the bottom of the saucepan or boil over, making an unnecessary mess of your cooker.

Another advantage of this recipe is that it goes a long way. It makes too much for one gift, so you can make two or three gifts at the same time. For fairs and bazaars you will easily be able to make up twenty generous packets, even after the family have all had their fill. I guarantee it will be a sure-fire hit at any such event and will sell out in no time.

Ingredients

250 g (8 oz) butter
500 ml (1 pint) milk
2 kg (4½ lbs) sugar
2 x 400 g (14 fl oz) tins condensed milk
30 ml (2 tbl) golden syrup
10 ml (2 tsp) vanilla essence

Method

1. Melt half the butter over a low heat.
2. Add the milk and the remaining butter. Add the sugar when all the butter has melted.
3. Stir constantly, ensuring that the sugar does not settle at the bottom of the saucepan.
4. As soon as the sugar mixture comes to the boil, add the condensed milk. Stir continuously to prevent the condensed milk from cooking too fast and forming brown bits in the mixture. Add the golden syrup while stirring. Stir the mixture every now and then until it comes to the boil. The heat should be low or the mixture will stick to the bottom of the saucepan.
5. Boil approximately 1-1½ hours or more depending on the saucepan and the specific cooker. Stir frequently. The fudge is ready as soon as the mixture has a dull appearance and makes big, heavy bubbles. It will also crystallize on a wooden spoon when the spoon is removed from the mixture. Drop some of the mixture on a saucer and test it with your finger or on your tongue. It should have a characteristic fudge texture.
6. Remove from the heat and quickly stir in the vanilla essence. Rapidly beat the mixture for a few minutes using a wooden spoon.
7. Quickly pour the mixture into a large 45 x 30 cm (18 x 11¾ in) and a small 21 x 34 cm (8¼ x 13¼ in) greased Swiss roll pan.
8. Allow the fudge to cool until the centre section begins to set. Cut into squares using a paring knife with a sharp, thin blade. Dip the blade in boiling water.
9. Allow the fudge to stand until it has cooled.
10. Use plastic sandwich bags to pack the fudge for fairs or small gifts, fastening each bag with a pretty ribbon. For Christmas, arrange the fudge on an attractively decorated paper plate. Wrap it in foil or cling film, or cover with a piece of cellophane and decorate with a large ribbon. Use a small basket or a pretty plate. If you're feeling very energetic, put it in a large bottle and make a fabric cover for the top to match the person's kitchen colour scheme. See page 27 for instructions on how to make the cover.

HINT

Allow the fudge to cool to room temperature before packing it away. This will prevent the packaging from becoming damp. Fudge also freezes very well. Make a batch, keep it in an airtight container in the freezer and use as a gift when the need suddenly arises. Be sure to keep it in a safe place or you might find that the rest of the family has left you with nothing but an empty container!

Coconut ice

Like fudge, coconut ice is a firm favourite with everyone. Yet one seldom sees it around these days and many of the recipes are laborious and expensive.

This recipe is quick, easy and relatively economical; the kids will be able to make it under supervision.

I always use a square 20 x 20 cm (8¾ x 8¾ in) glass dish for making it. Because it's deeper than a tin it produces beautifully tall squares. A similar dish should yield approximately forty-nine 2-cm (¾ in) high squares.

Ingredients

25 g (1 oz) butter
375 ml (¾ pt) milk
800 g (1¾ lbs) sugar
160 g (6 oz) coconut
5 ml (1 tsp) vanilla essence
5 drops red food colouring

Method

1. Melt the butter in a heavy based saucepan and add the milk and sugar.
2. Stir the milk mixture until it comes to the boil.
3. Simmer over a low heat for 15 minutes without stirring.
4. Remove the saucepan from the stove and allow the mixture to cool.
5. Beat the milk mixture thoroughly using a wooden spoon and add the coconut and vanilla essence. Work rapidly after adding the coconut to prevent the mixture from setting in the saucepan.
6. Pour half the mixture into a greased metal or glass dish.
7. Add the food colouring to the remaining half of the mixture and stir thoroughly to obtain an even colour.
8. Pour the pink mixture on top of the white mixture in the tin or dish.
9. Allow the coconut ice to cool thoroughly and then cut into squares using a paring knife with a sharp, thin blade. Dip the blade in boiling water every now and then.
10. Leave the coconut ice to stand for a few more hours before removing it from the tin or dish.
11. Arrange the coconut ice on a sturdy paper plate or in a small basket and cover with cling film or a piece of cellophane. Decorate the parcel with a pretty ribbon. Coconut ice is quite brittle and should preferably not be packed loose in a plastic bag as it will disintegrate completely.

HINT

When making coconut ice for a Christmas gift, colour the second half pale green instead of pink. It looks marvellous when arranged on a paper plate and decorated with Christmas baubles and green, red and white ribbons.

Dorette's crunchies

Everyone is familiar with crunchies made from oats and baked in a Swiss roll tin before being cut into squares. They are delicious, but unfortunately they soon become stale and lose their crunchy texture.

This recipe is also for oat cookies, the only difference being that they remain beautifully fresh and crunchy. They go down a treat with all ages and, served with tea or cocoa, they are a perfect bedtime snack.

These biscuits freeze very well — simply pack them into plastic bags or containers — and quickly regain room temperature. Always keep some handy, as they make a most welcome gift for someone at home or in the hospital who is not feeling well, or for new mothers along with a gift for the baby.

Ingredients

280 g (10 oz) plain flour
160 g (6 oz) coconut
160 g (6 oz) oats
5 ml (1 tsp) salt
250 g (8 oz) margarine
400 g (14 oz) sugar
30 ml (2 tbl) golden syrup
10 ml (2 tsp) bicarbonate of soda
45 ml (3 tbl) boiling water
1 egg
5 ml (1 tsp) vanilla essence

Method

1. Preheat the oven to 180 °C (350 °F/Gas 4).
2. Mix together in a bowl the flour, coconut, oats and salt.
3. Melt together the margarine, sugar and syrup on the stove.
4. Dissolve the bicarbonate of soda in the boiling water and add to the margarine mixture.
5. Beat the egg and add it to the margarine mixture, together with the vanilla essence.
6. Add the margarine mixture to the dry ingredients and mix well.
7. Roll the dough into small balls, place them on a greased baking tray and flatten slightly.
8. Bake for approximately 12 minutes until the cookies are golden brown.

> **HINT**
>
> *To make really nourishing cookies, substitute half the flour with wholemeal flour, the sugar with brown sugar and the golden syrup with honey. Also add 30-45 ml (2-3 tbl) sesame seed.*

Easy yeast rusks

One of my aims in life was to master the art of baking delicious yeast rusks just like those of my Aunt Santjie on the farm. However, I soon gave up all hope, as the recipe was not only difficult and involved, but one also had to give up a night's sleep in the process.

Fortunately my friend Alida came across this easy, modern recipe for rusks that look and taste exactly like their old-fashioned counterparts. Now we and everyone who has begged us for the recipe always have a batch in stock. As a matter of interest, Alida was given a bag of these rusks as a gift and immediately asked for the recipe as well. So if you're planning it as a gift it's a good idea to provide the recipe in advance!

Ingredients
500 g (18 oz) butter
150 ml (6 fl oz) condensed milk diluted with 300 ml
(12 fl oz) water
50 ml (3 fl oz) milk
480 g (1 lb) sugar
3 eggs
1 cake yeast
2.5 kg (5 lb) plain flour

Method
EVENING
1. Melt the butter in a large saucepan and add the milk and sugar. Heat the mixture until all the sugar has dissolved and leave until lukewarm.
2. Beat the eggs and add to the lukewarm milk mixture.
3. Crumble the yeast cake in the milk and egg mixture.
4. Sprinkle 280 g (10 oz) of the 2.5 kg (5 lb) flour over the yeast mixture and beat with a fork.
5. Cover the saucepan and leave in a warm place for the mixture to rise. This will take about 20 minutes; the mixture is ready when the surface is covered with tiny bubbles.
6. Sieve the remaining flour into a very large mixing bowl for kneading.

7. Add the yeast mixture plus 500 ml (1 pt) lukewarm water to the flour. Mix the flour and the liquid and knead until the dough is nicely manageable. The dough is ready when it easily comes away from your hands and has a satiny texture.
8. Lightly cover the bowl containing the dough with cling film — leave sufficient room for the dough to rise — and wrap the entire bowl in a heavy tablecloth or blanket. Leave the dough in a warm place overnight to rise.

NEXT MORNING
Don't rush. Take your time and enjoy your breakfast before tackling the rusks.
9. Grease three large baking trays with butter or lard.
10. Slightly beat down the risen dough and divide it in three.
11. Between the palms of your hands, roll balls half the height of the tins and arrange in rows of three.
12. When the three pans are filled with balls of dough, leave the dough in a warm place to rise again until double its original height. This should take about half an hour or even longer.
13. Preheat the oven to 180 °C (350 °F/Gas 4).
14. Bake the risen rusks for approximately 50 minutes until pale brown.
15. If you like, brush the tops of the rusks with a strong solution of sugar water 10 minutes before they are due to come out of the oven.
16. Turn the rusks out and break into pieces as soon as they are cool enough to handle.
17. Dry the rusks for about 12 hours at 100 °C (212 °F/Gas ¼).
18. Pack them in large plastic bags or airtight containers and decorate with a ribbon.

> **HINT**
> *Any yeast recipe rises beautifully in an oven that's been heated at 100 °C (212 °F/Gas ¼) for a few minutes and then switched off.*

Muesli

Who would have thought that cereal could make such a welcome gift. You can't give my sister a more welcome gift, for example. This practical breakfast food is deliciously nutritious and, if you have about 75 ml (4 oz) of it with yoghurt or milk for breakfast, you'll keep the hunger pangs at bay for hours.

The biggest task when preparing this gift is to get all the ingredients together, but a large supermarket should have everything you need in stock.

The recipe is enough for a large mixing bowl. So make sure that you have a container that's big enough. It can also be stored in airtight containers in the freezer. Use the muesli as required as it does not need defrosting.

Ingredients
500 g (18 oz) wheat flakes
300 g (10 oz) wheat germ
500 g (18 oz) oats
500 g (18 oz) finely ground, unsalted peanuts or other nuts
45 ml (3 tbl) yeast powder
500 g (18 oz) Grape Nuts
500 g (18 oz) sultanas or raisins
200 g (6 oz) bran
300 g (10 oz) instant skim milk powder
200 g (8 oz) brown sugar

Method
1. Preheat the oven to 100 °C (212 °F/Gas ¼).
2. Bake the dry oats on a baking tray for 15 minutes. Take care that it does not burn. The oats are done when they no longer have a characteristic raw taste.
3. Grind the nuts and wheat flakes in a food processor until fine.
4. Once the oats are cool, mix all the ingredients together in a large mixing bowl.
5. Pack the muesli in plastic bags fastened with a pretty ribbon or in a bottle with a covered top. See page 27 for instructions on how to make a pretty cover.

> **HINT**
> *Because it's easy to carry in a backpack, muesli makes a perfect gift for someone who enjoys hiking. It's light and does not make a mess. If it's to be used on a camping trip, double the amount of milk powder; then simply add water for a delicious and filling breakfast.*

CHAPTER 2

Gifts from the garden

The countryside, the garden or any flower is a gift in itself, which is why making a gift using plants is so rewarding. But, unless it is a potted plant, such a gift is temporary, as flowers eventually wither and have to be thrown away.

The gifts discussed in this chapter are all examples of how plants can be enjoyed for longer than usual by drying them. In addition, potpourri has the advantage that it not only looks good, but gives off a lovely fragrance. Once the art of drying flowers has been mastered, the possibility of gifts made from them is virtually endless. You can use these ideas to spark off some of your own, and you may want to experiment with various types of plant material.

17

Potpourri

It's fun making potpourri and once you've discovered the magic of aromatic plants, your garden and the countryside will gain a new dimension. The first time I arrived home with a few sweet-smelling bunches, the rest of the family took little notice. However, they too soon discovered their magical properties. When one breaks off and crushes a leaf in passing or even just waters the plants, one can hardly believe it possible for them to be so fragrant. On a recent ramble along a nature trail, my husband was amazed by the heady fragrances of some of the indigenous plants. He now believes that one instinctively recognises a sweet-smelling bush.

To make potpourri does not mean you have to start your garden from scratch. You might like to add a couple of plants, but use what's available. Indigenous plants include a wealth of aromatic herbs and bushes. Experiment with different combinations, using both aromatic and colourful plants, especially when making potpourri for a glass container.

There are a number of traditional plants that are often used for making potpourri.

Few gardens do not boast at least one rose bush. You might even be fortunate enough to have a few old-fashioned rose bushes; their blooms are often more fragrant than those of the new varieties.

There are also quite a few well-known lavender bushes (*Lavandula* species). The leaves or flowers of these bushes have a characteristic sharp, fragrant smell. Harvest the flowers when the top flowers start opening. I use the dried flowers on their own in order to make little sweet-smelling potpourri sachet bags and put the leaves into potpourri.

Another plant with an amazing fragrance which grows very easily is the lemon verbena (*Aloysia triphylla*). It makes a most attractive bush that loses its flowers in winter. The leaves dry quickly and have a sharp scent.

There are also many kinds of geranium (*Pelargonium* species) with aromatic leaves that make superb potpourri ingredients when dried. Other plants that have heady fragrances are rosemary — an old favourite — santolina, garden pink and jasmine.

Blue or purple dried flowers give any potpourri an attractive appearance. A few dried Petrea flowers or blue Agapanthus flowers can be used to good effect. Pick the large Agapanthus flowers for an arrangement in the home and use the tiny flowers that dry on the inside of the umbel for the potpourri. If they dry outside, they lose some of their colour.

In addition to the dried materials, essential oils, fixatives and spices are used in potpourri. The essential oils are the pleasant fragrances of flowers or something else that smell good in a bottle, while the fixatives, namely orris powder and dried orange peel, ensure that the fragrance of the flowers and the essential oils are preserved longer. The spices help to impart a special fragrance to the mixture.

OLGA KERSTEN'S POTPOURRI RECIPE

Ingredients
Approximately 5 ml (1 tsp) essential oil
50 g (2 oz) orris powder
Dried peel of 2 oranges
Approximately 50 g (2 oz) spices
Approximately 2.5 ℓ (5 pt) dried plant material
A small glass jar
A large glass bottle with a tight-fitting lid

Method
1. Peel the oranges and dry the peel on a cake rack in a warm place. The peel will harden and must be broken into small pieces, using a hammer if necessary.
2. Make your own spice mixture using, for example, the following spices: whole cinnamon, whole cloves, star aniseed; or buy a ready-made mixture. The proportion and quantities of the different spices will depend on your own taste. Some people; for instance, like the aroma of cloves, while others don't. Gently crush the spices slightly in a mortar or tap them with a hammer.
3. Add the orris powder, the dried orange peel and the

mixture of spices to the small glass jar. Add approximately 5 ml (1 tsp) of the essential oil of your choice and mix well. It's a good idea to start off with a blended oil — one that contains a mixture of different fragrances. Initially, this mixture won't have a fragrant aroma, but cover it tightly and leave for approximately two weeks to ripen. Thereafter, you can add more oil or spices.

4. In the meantime, dry the plant material as follows: pick the material early in the morning once all the dew has evaporated. The drier the atmosphere, the better.

Always dry the material in a warm, dry room or airing cupboard and never in the sun. With some plants, such as lavender, you can tie small branches into bunches and hang them upside down. Other plant material, like rose petals, should be dried on cooling racks covered with plastic mosquito netting. The more air that is allowed to circulate around the material, the sooner and better it will dry. Once the material is brittle, it is ready for use.

5. Add the already prepared mixture in the small glass jar to the bottom of the large glass bottle and add the dried plant material. For the plant material mixture, use what's available according to your own taste. Cover tightly and shake the bottle well. Leave to mature in the bottle for approximately four weeks. Try to shake the bottle every day.

6. When ready, fill little bags as sachets, or fill delicate bowls with the potpourri.

HINT

Transfer the essential oil from the bottle it comes in to a clean, dry bottle with a dropper. Use the dropper to drop some of the fragrant oil on anything you want to give a sweet scent to. Stale potpourri can also be revived with a few drops of oil.

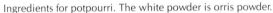

Ingredients for potpourri. The white powder is orris powder.

Wreaths and decorated hats

This wreath or hat will always attract admiring second glances. Yet both items are quick and easy to make. The hat in the photograph is decorated with three bunches of flowers and ribbons, but it will look equally pretty with a wreath to fit around the crown.

Requirements

Fabric flowers or dried everlastings on wire stems
Dried gypsophila (Baby's breath)
Starflowers
Green or white florist's tape
Satin ribbon 5-7 mm (¼-⅜ in) wide for the ordinary bows and 15 mm (¾ in) wide for the extra bow on the hat and the long tail ends for the wreath
Clear glue

For the hat you will also need:
A straw hat
Narrow lace

Method

1. Dry the gypsophila by hanging bunches of it upside down in an airy room. Take care not to dry them in the sun.

2. Cut 8 cm (3 in) of florist's tape for each bunch of flowers you'll be making.

3. Arrange the flowers in bunches – place an everlasting or a few fabric flowers in the centre of the gypsophila, surrounded by starflowers – and cover 6 cm (2½ in) of the stems with florist's tape. Part of the wire stem of the large flower will still be left uncovered, but do not cut it off. Make as many bunches as you require for your specific size wreath or hat. You will need approximately nine bunches of flowers for a wreath, while the number for the hat depends on your taste.

4. Tie the bunches of flowers together using florist's tape. Take the first bunch and position the second one on top of its covered stem, leaving a 5-mm (¼ in) space between the first and second bunch of flowers for a bow to be glued on later. Tie the two bunches together with approximately 6 cm (2½ in) of florist's tape cut in advance. Repeat this process with each bunch of flowers. If you're making a wreath, shape it so that the first and the last bunches meet. If necessary, shorten some of the stems on the large flowers to prevent the wire base of the wreath from becoming too heavy. Finally, fold the stems of the last bunch of flowers underneath the first bunch of flowers and secure them. If you want to decorate a hat all around its crown, ensure that the wreath is the correct size.

5. This step applies to hats only. Measure two lengths of lace: one to go around the bottom of the crown and one for the edge of the hat brim. Apply glue around the bottom of the crown. Position the flowers and glue the lace to the hat. Repeat for the brim.

6. Make as many bows, of about 6 cm (2½ in) in diameter, as required. Remember to finish the ends by cutting them diagonally across or in a V-shape, and seal (see hint on page 27). Glue a bow between every pair of flower bunches on the wreath. You can glue as many as three bows with 45-cm (18 in) long tails to the centre of the back of the hat – one on the wreath and the other two to the hat itself, above and below the first bow. For the final touch, secure extra ribbon to the centre back of the wreath's wire base.

7. If you are decorating a hat, not a wreath, even more bows can be glued to the hat itself, depending on your taste.

HINT
Make special herb bags for the linen cupboard by filling them with dried santolina, lemon verbena and lavender leaves. The linen will smell wonderfully fresh, and you will never again be plagued by insects.

A posy of dried flowers

I'm convinced many a girl's heart has melted when she is presented with one of these beautiful posies that my friend Bev makes with such loving care.

Requirements
Dried hydrangeas
Dried everlastings with wire stems
Fine dried gypsophila (Baby's breath)
Starflowers
Green florist's tape
80 cm (32 in) grey curling ribbon — 5 mm (¼ in) wide
50 cm (20 in) narrow satin ribbon — 5 mm (¼ in) wide
White tissue paper or cellophane

Method
1. Pick the hydrangeas when they have stopped flowering and start turning green. Dry them by tying them in bunches and hang them upside down in an airy room. Dry the gypsophila in the same way. Avoid drying them in the sun.

2. Use one large hydrangea flower and insert a few everlastings among the smaller hydrangea flowers. Hold all the stems in your free hand.

3. Now carefully insert the starflowers, a few at a time, amongst the small hydrangea flowers. If there are too many, remove them. Pull the starflowers out a little; they should protrude above the other flowers.

4. Insert pieces of gypsophila among the other flowers to make a full bunch and secure the stems with florist's tape.

5. Make a single bunch for a small posy. Use two bunches for a large posy.

6. For an even larger posy, put the three bunches together to make a neat triangular shape. Close any gaps that still show between the bunches with more everlastings, starflowers and gypsophila. Secure all the stems with florist's tape.

7. Tie the curling ribbon around the 'throat' of the posy and fashion a bow. Curl the loose ends.

8. Place the posy diagonally across a piece of tissue paper or cellophane and cut off a square large enough for the posy to fit diagonally across it.

9. Fold the two free corners of the square together and wrap the stems. Fasten the paper or cellophane with tape.

10. Using the satin ribbon, tie a bow around the paper or cellophane and the stems. Finish the ribbon ends with V-shaped notches.

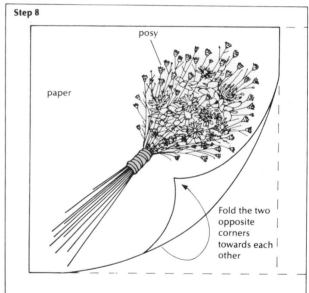

Step 8

posy

paper

Fold the two opposite corners towards each other

HINT
Put a drop of essential oil on the flowers to give them a fragrant aroma.

CHAPTER 3
Gifts from the sewing basket

The gifts in this chapter are made by sewing, but you do not need to be a highly competent seamstress to make them all. A good measure of interest and enthusiasm is all that is required. If you've never done needlework before, don't become disheartened. Choose an easy project to start with. Follow the instructions carefully, and even your first attempt should be successful. Then, hopefully, you will be so inspired that more will follow. Use the best quality fabric you can afford and work as neatly as possible. To begin, a metre of cream cotton sheeting, a few metres of cream satin ribbon and a couple of metres of cotton lace go a long way. Cream is a colour that blends with most others, and the fabric is extremely wide, so you can use it for many different items.

EQUIPMENT FOR THE SEWING BASKET

Trying to sew without a few basic pieces of equipment is very frustrating and could easily dampen your enthusiasm. Equip yourself with some basic tools before starting a project. It's an investment for life and a one-off expenditure.

1. A decent pair of scissors is essential. It is impossible to work with blunt scissors that have seen better days, and you can end up ruining and wasting fabric. Several companies make excellent ranges of scissors that are a pleasure to use and are widely available. It's useful to have a large pair of scissors for general use (1) and a small pair of sharp-pointed needlework scissors (2) — the entire household will put them to good use. A piece of equipment that many people may not be familiar with is the Scissors Tuner (3) — a flat metal square that's so small it fits into a purse. I guarantee you that it works perfectly. Even the bluntest scissors work like new when sharpened with it.

There are also special scissors available for left-handed people (4). If you cannot find them on the shelf, the retailer can easily order them from the distributors. My sister is left-handed and life was made so much easier for her the day she was given a pair of scissors for left-handed people — she never dreamed that it would be so easy to cut using her left hand!

2. An air-soluble marking pen (5) is the second most important piece of equipment. This is a wonderful invention that makes it that much easier and more fun to sew. It can be used to make as many marks as you wish on your fabric, because they disappear as if by magic after a while. With some fabrics, it might take a little longer, but all signs of any marks you make actually do vanish, usually within an hour or so. We even use them to make marks on our walls when hanging pictures — they are absolutely ideal.

3. To complement the air-soluble pen, you should get a pen that makes water-soluble marks (6) — when the marked item is dunked in water, the marks disappear.

4. A transparent ruler (7) measuring at least 30 cm (12 in) is indispensable and is used for just about every item in the book.

5. Thin steel pins (8) 3.5cm (1½ in) long are another must. Once you've become accustomed to working with them, you'll never be able to use the shorter pins again.

Covers for bottle tops

In many households the attractive glass bottles and jars that chutney, jam, mayonnaise, etc. come in are thrown away. However, if you make your own gifts, this will never happen. Instead, those same bottles and jars can be used for packing homemade or even bought sweets, biscuits and muesli. And if you make a cheerful cover in cotton fabric for its top, even the most ordinary bottle is suddenly transformed into a beautiful gift.

Single bottle top covers are most suitable for smaller jars, while their bigger counterparts look best in double covers. A very striking effect is achieved by using striped fabric and positioning the stripes at right angles (for double covers). When selecting fabric, ensure that it is not too heavy or too stiff — a thin fabric is more suitable.

Requirements
Pieces of plain or printed cotton fabric
Lace
Approximately 75 cm (2½ ft) satin ribbon for each bottle
A reel of thin, round elastic
Compasses and pencil

Measurements for different bottle sizes:
(Adapt these for each specific type of bottle.)

Type of bottle	Diameter of lid	Diameter of fabric	Diameter of elastic stitching
Medicine	3 cm (1¼ in)	10 cm (4 in)	8 cm (3¼ in)
Jam	7.5 cm (3 in)	15 cm (6 in)	10 cm (4 in)
Mayonnaise	7 cm (2¾ in)	15-19 cm (6-7½ in)	11 cm (8½ in)
Chutney	8.5 cm (3½ in)	16-20 cm (6½-8 in)	13 cm (7 in)

Method
1. Draw circles with the appropriate diameters on paper and cut them out. Mark the centre of the circles by making a small hole in the paper.

2. Cut out fabric circles and mark the centre of each circle by inserting the air-soluble pen through the hole on the pattern. Zigzag the edges of the circles.
3. Zigzag the ungathered lace on top of the finished edge of the circle. The circles will be crooked at first, but once they are gathered, they will take on the correct shape.
4. To make a double cover, carefully pin the two circles on top of one another so that the centres correspond.
5. Using compasses and pencil or air-soluble pen, mark the line along which the elastic is to be stitched.
6. Using the buttonhole foot of the machine, insert one end of the elastic through the hole in the foot from the front. Pin this end to the fabric. Stitch across the elastic with narrow, short zigzag stitches, using the left hand to pull the elastic tight from the front. Never wind the elastic on the bottom bobbin of your machine unless you have a special bobbin for elastic, or you are certain that your machine can handle elastic. The elastic could affect the tension setting of your machine.
7. Once the stitched circle has been completed, cut off the elastic and pull it tighter if necessary. Knot the two ends tightly together, ensuring that the knot will not come undone. Neatly tie off the loose threads with which it was stitched.
8. Pull the cover over the bottle top (fill the bottle in advance), and tie a pretty ribbon around the top to finish it off.
9. Cut the ends of the ribbon at an angle and seal them as described below.

> **HINT**
> *The raw ends of satin ribbon can be sealed by burning them carefully with a match or by pressing them down on a hot hob.*

Lavender dolls

From a young age most little girls simply love sweet-smelling things and dolls, so these lavender dolls are a real treat. The dolls are so easy to make that in no time you can build up a whole stock of them. Older girls will easily be able to make the dolls themselves.

Requirements
Paper for patterns
12 x 20 cm (5 x 8 in) piece of cotton print fabric
9 x 9 cm (4 x 4 in) piece of white cotton fabric
42 cm (18 in) narrow ribbon
Approximately 40 cm (16 in) narrow white lace
A wooden bead, 3 cm (1¼ in) in diameter
Brown, pink and red acrylic paint
A very fine paintbrush
Dried lavender flowers or potpourri (see page 18 for recipe)

Method
1. From paper, cut out a 12 x 20-cm (5 x 8 in) rectangle and a circle 8 cm (3¼ in) in diameter to use as patterns for cutting out the fabric.
2. Using the patterns, cut out a rectangle on the printed fabric and a circle on the white fabric.
3. With the air-soluble pen, draw a line parallel to the bottom edge of the printed fabric, 3 cm (1¼ in) from the edge. Stitch a piece of ribbon 20 cm (8 in) long to this line. Zigzag side edges and top edge of the piece of fabric.
4. Fold the fabric in half with right sides facing and stitch a seam 1 cm (½ in) wide, leaving an opening in the seam as indicated on the diagram.
5. Open the seam and fold the bag as indicated on the diagram. Stitch the bottom opening, allowing 50 mm (¼ in) for the seam. Zigzag the seam edges. Fold 1 cm (½ in) of the top edge of the bag to the wrong side.
6. Using a double thread, tack small stitches 2 mm (¹⁄₁₆ in) from the top edge of the bag. Close by pulling the thread tight and tying a knot. Sew up the top and tie off the loose ends of the thread.
7. Zigzag the edge of the white circle of fabric and zigzag a gathered piece of lace to the edge.

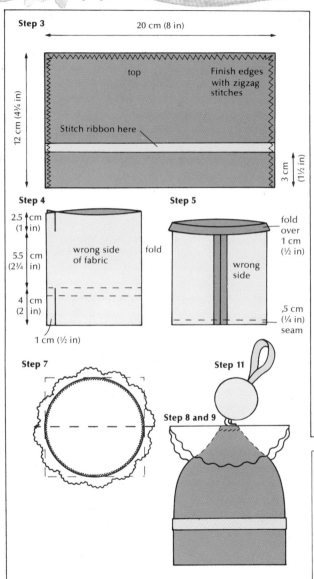

Step 3

20 cm (8 in)

12 cm (4¾ in)

top

Finish edges with zigzag stitches

Stitch ribbon here

3 cm (1½ in)

Step 4

2.5 cm (1 in)

5.5 cm (2¾ in)

wrong side of fabric

fold

4 cm (2 in)

1 cm (½ in)

Step 5

fold over 1 cm (½ in)

wrong side

,5 cm (¼ in) seam

Step 7

Step 11

Step 8 and 9

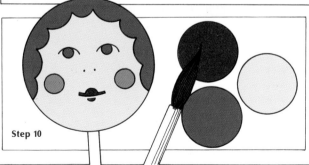

Step 10

8. Fold the white fabric in half with wrong sides facing and sew the centre of the fold to the centre of the bag's gathered edge.

9. Fold the remaining 22 cm (10 in) ribbon in half. Seal the ends and sew them firmly to the centre of the white collar to form a loop.

10. Insert a stick or pipecleaner into the hole in the bead to hold it steady. First paint the hair and then the eyes and nose, using the brown paint. Use pink paint for the cheeks and paint the mouth in red.

11. Leave the paint to dry thoroughly and thread the bead onto the ribbon loop. Push it firmly down onto the white collar. If the hole in the bead is so large that the bead might slip off, insert a small piece of wood in the hole to secure it.

12. From any fine material or very fine net make a small bag measuring 5 x 5 cm (2 x 2 in) and stuff it with dried lavender flowers or potpourri, through the opening left in the seam. If you have plenty of lavender flowers or potpourri in stock, stuff the entire dress and close the opening with oversewing.

HINT
These dolls also make wonderful Christmas tree decorations. Use red, green or Christmas fabric for their dresses.

Victorian lace decorations

Any girl, young or old, will be delighted with one of these enchanting Victorian lace decorations as a gift.

Requirements

A wooden embroidery hoop — oval frames are just as pretty
Net, lace or voile curtain fabric to stretch over the hoop
Wide lace — approximately 2 to 2½ times the circumference of the hoop
Scraps of lace, ribbon, etc. for decoration
Satin ribbon to hang up the hoop with and to glue around the outer edge approximately 2 times the circumference of the frame
Liquid glue
Typing paper

Method

1. Sew ribbon, lace or any other decoration of your choice to the net, lace or voile. The flowers on the large decoration in the photograph are made from lace which has been gathered into circles and then sewn to the voile by hand, with fine stitches.
2. Stretch the fabric very tightly over the frame and cut it away around the circumference of the frame, leaving a 1-cm (½ in) edge.
3. Apply glue to the back of the outer ring of the frame. Leave the glue for a few minutes to become tacky.
4. Fold the edge of fabric out and press down on the glued edge with your fingers. Repeat this until the fabric lies flat on the wood. Leave the glue to dry.
5. Cut off the excess fabric close to the frame with sharp scissors.
6. Gather the wide lace — either pull a thread of the lace itself or stitch along the straight edge of the lace and gather it.
7. Machine stitch the evenly gathered lace to a piece of paper along the gathered edge. Remove the paper from the lace. The lace will now be stable enough to work

with. Without the paper the lace will crumple up and become difficult to space evenly.
8. Apply glue to the entire back of the embroidery frame, including the fabric that has already been glued to the frame. Leave the glue to become tacky.
9. With the right side facing down, glue the lace to the frame. Start opposite the screw on the frame and fold the lace back 1 cm (½ in); the front will now be finished. Use the division between the two rings as a guide. I try to glue the edge of the lace or the stitching to this division. Press down firmly and if necessary insert pins at right angles on the frame to keep the lace in position. Finish off by cutting the lace 1 cm (½ in) beyond the beginning and glueing it over the beginning. Leave to dry thoroughly.
10. Measure a length of ribbon to glue to the outer edge of the frame, ie the edge that will be visible from the side, and seal the ends of the ribbon. A brightly coloured ribbon often complements the decoration.
11. Put a little glue on a piece of paper and leave to become tacky.
12. Apply the tacky glue to the outer edge of the embroidery frame.
13. Glue the ribbon to the edge of the frame with one edge of the ribbon exactly on the front edge of the embroidery frame. Too much glue may make grease marks on the ribbon. Leave the glue to dry thoroughly.
14. The decoration can be adorned in various ways where the screw is situated.

- Fold the ribbon to be used for hanging the decoration and tie a knot approximately 30 cm (12 in) from the ends. This makes a loop from which to hang the frame. Insert the loose ends of the ribbon through the opening below the screw of the frame. Bring the loose ends to the front and make a pretty bow. To make a triple bow like the one on the large decoration, make two loops in one end and one in the other and tie them once as for an ordinary bow.
- Take a length of ribbon twice as long as the

hanging loop. Tie the ends and insert the loop from behind through the opening below the screw. Glue a small bow and a few flowers to the frame below the screw.

• Make a loop as described above. Make a posy of dried flowers, and leave a few bows and ribbons to hang over the flowers and the tightly stretched fabric. Sew the posy, bows and ribbons to the fabric around the screw.

HINTS

☐ If you have only narrow lace, you can widen it by stitching two lengths together on top of one another with the scalloped edge of the one piece positioned on top of the straight edge of the other.

☐ For an even more unusual decoration, position potpourri between two layers of net and stretch both layers over the frame.

Hearts galore

Stuffed fabric hearts can be used for making a wide variety of gifts. Only a small piece of fabric is required for each heart; so it's an ideal way to use up bits of leftover cotton fabric.

INSTRUCTIONS FOR MAKING HEARTS

Requirements
Cotton fabric
Polyester wadding
A small pair of sharp-pointed scissors

Please note: The pattern appears on page 87.

Method
1. Trace the motif on a piece of paper or cardboard and use it as a pattern for cutting out two pieces of material for each heart — 5 mm (¼ in) is allowed for the seams.
2. With right sides facing, stitch along the edge, allowing 5 mm (¼ in) for the seam. Start at the bottom right, near the point of the heart, and end approximately 2.5 cm (1 in) from the point. Do not begin and end with double stitching; finish off by firmly knotting the threads. Bear in mind that double stitching changes the shape of the hearts.
3. Cut small notches all around the heart, 3 mm (⅛ in) apart and nearly right against the seam stitching, except near the opening, which is used for stuffing the heart. Use small, very sharp-pointed scissors to cut the notches.
4. Turn the heart inside out, stuff firmly with wadding and sew up the opening using tiny slip stitches.

A wreath of hearts for the kitchen
Add dried herbs and spices to the wadding used for stuffing the hearts. Make a magnificent wreath for a friend's kitchen with the hearts.

Requirements
Green vines or a grapevine wreath
9 stuffed hearts
9 pieces of stick cinnamon
1 m (1 yd) wide satin ribbon, 2.5 cm (1 in) wide
3 m (3 yd) narrow satin ribbon, 6 mm (¼ in) wide
Thin florist's wire

Method
1. To make a wreath, remove the leaves (not the tendrils) from the grapevines. Plait a wreath by making a circle 35 cm (14 in) in diameter with one of the vines. Twist the rest of the vine and the other vines around this circle. If the vines are dried and hard, soften by soaking them in water.

2. Leave the wreath in a warm place to dry. This will take a week or two.

3. Make the hearts according to the instructions on page 32 and stuff with dried aromatic herbs and spices only or a mixture of herbs, spices and wadding.

4. Cut nine 32-cm (13-in) pieces of narrow satin ribbon, and tie a bow around each piece of stick cinnamon. Cut the ends of the ribbon at an angle and seal them.

5. Wrap the wide ribbon around the wreath and sew the ends together at the back.

6. Position the hearts evenly around the wreath and sew them to the wreath using a double thread. Insert the needle through the wreath from the back of the wreath and into the back of a heart. Then insert the needle from the front of the wreath to the back. Tie the thread firmly around a few vines and cut, leaving short ends of thread. Tie each heart in at least two places to secure it properly.

7. Insert a piece of florist's wire at the back of a stick of cinnamon, between the cinnamon and the ribbon. Position on the wreath and twist the wire firmly around one of the vines. Cut the wire neatly.

8. Insert dried flowers into the wreath.

A bunch of sweet-smelling hearts

A bunch of sweet-smelling hearts looks charming anywhere. Stuff them with dried herbs and spices if they are for a kitchen, and with potpourri for a bedroom or bathroom.

Requirements
5 stuffed hearts
3.2 m (3½ yds) narrow satin ribbon, 5 mm (¼ in) wide
A curtain ring, 2.5 cm (1 in) in diameter

Method
1. Make the hearts as shown on page 32 and stuff them according to taste.

2. Cut five 28-cm (11 in) pieces of ribbon and tie bows 8 cm (3¼ in) in diameter (see hint on page 34). Cut the ends of the ribbon at an angle and seal them.

3. Cut another piece of ribbon measuring 20 cm (8 in) and tie a bow 5 cm (2 in) in diameter for the ring.

4. Cut the remaining ribbon in the following lengths: 13, 21, 29, 37 and 45 cm (5, 8¼, 11½, 15 and 18 in). Seal the ends of the ribbons and sew one end of each ribbon and one bow made in step 2 to each heart.

5. Layer the ribbons from the longest to the shortest on top of one another. The loose ends should be even. Tack them together with a stitch or two. Insert 1 cm (½ in) of this end through the ring and anchor it with a few stitches. Sew the small bow to the front of the long ribbons, just below the ring.

Hearts for a newborn baby

Make some brightly coloured toys for a newborn baby by combining stuffed hearts and bells.

Requirements
3 stuffed hearts in brightly coloured cotton fabric
4.3 m (4¾ yd) narrow satin ribbon
6 small bells

Method
1. Make the hearts as shown on page 32.

2. Cut six 28-cm (11 in) pieces of ribbon and tie them in bows 8 cm (3¼ in) in diameter (see hint on page 34). Cut the ends at an angle and seal them.

3. Firmly sew a bow with a bell on top on either side of the V of each heart.

4. Sew the hearts together at their curves, using firm stitching.

5. Cut the remaining ribbon into two pieces and sew the centre of each piece to the outer curves of the two hearts on the outside. Use this ribbon to tie the toy across the cot or pram.

A pincushion for the wrist

A pincushion on a wristband is extremely useful.

Requirements

One stuffed heart
Cotton fabric to match the heart 6 x 30 cm (2½ x 12 in)
40 cm (16 in) elastic, 5 mm (¼ in) wide

Method

1. Follow the instructions on page 32 to make the heart.
2. Fold the fabric for the wristband in half lengthwise with right sides together. Stitch, allowing 1 cm (½ in) for the seam.

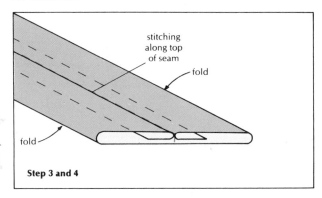

stitching along top of seam

fold

fold

Step 3 and 4

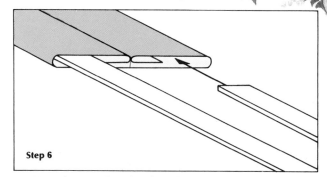

Step 6

3. Turn the wristband right side out and iron it flat with the seam lying exactly in the centre of one of the flat sides.
4. Make two channels in the wristband by stitching along the top of the seam.
5. Cut the elastic into two pieces. If possible, measure it around the wrist of the person for whom it is intended.
6. Insert each piece of elastic through one of the channels in the wristband and firmly sew each end to the ends of the wristband.
7. Turn the ends of the wristband back 5 mm (¼ in) and position them so that they lie between the back of the heart and the rest of the wristband. Firmly slip stitch the wristband to the heart, ensuring that the turned-back ends are not visible. (See picture on p. 26.)

HINT

Pretty bows of different sizes can be made by driving two nails into a plank a certain distance apart – eg 4 cm (1½ in), 5 cm (2½ in), etc. – depending on the diameter of the bow. Hook the ribbon, with the right side facing out, around the two nails. Make a bow in the middle between two nails by folding the one end beneath and then above the back ribbon, and then tying the two ends with a knot. Remove from the nails.

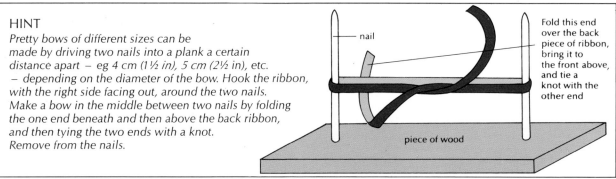

nail

Fold this end over the back piece of ribbon, bring it to the front above, and tie a knot with the other end

piece of wood

Glasses case

A pretty glasses case in bright cotton print will be popular with one and all. Leftover fabric can be used, so it is very economical. While you are at it, you can make a few at a time. By using different coloured ribbon, lace, beads and bells, you can make several from the same fabric, each with a different finish.

Requirements

1 piece of thin foam, 10 x 41 cm (4 x 16½ in)
2 pieces of cotton print, each measuring
*   10 x 41 cm (4 x 16½ in)*
1 piece of cotton print, 3.5 x 11 cm (1½ x 4 ½ in)
65 cm (26 in) bias binding (cotton, if possible)
1 large press stud
Lace, ribbon, beads and bells for decoration
An air-soluble pen

Method

1. Cut out a foam rectangle 10 x 41 cm (4 x 16½ in) — ensure that the corners are exactly square.
2. Using the foam as pattern, cut out two pieces of fabric. It creates a most interesting effect if you use different kinds of toning fabric for the inside and outside of the bag. Don't use fabric in very pale colours as the bag will be handled frequently and will soon become dirty.
3. Fold the two pieces of fabric to both sides of the foam. Make sure that the right sides face out.
4. Zigzag the fabric and foam together all along the edges.
5. Decide how you would like to quilt the fabric and mark the quilting lines with an air-soluble pen on the outside of the bag. For example, diagonal lines, vertical lines, diamond shapes and squares can be quilted on the case.
6. Stitch through on the right side using a long stitch setting and a thick needle (80-90). Try to limit the number of times you finish off — the stitching comes

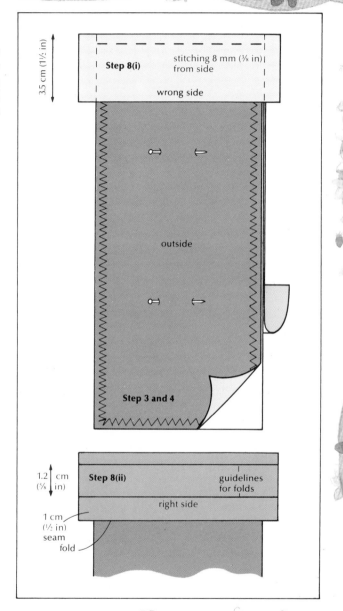

undone easily at these points and the case will not look neat. Tie a knot in the threads at this point or stitch backwards and forwards a few times.

7. Sew on all the ribbon and lace decorations at this point.

8. Pipe one short edge as follows:

Put the third small piece of fabric, with the wrong side up, on the outside of the bag against the short edge of the bag that will lie underneath the flap. Stitch 8 mm (⅜ in) from the edge (i). Then fold the piece of fabric up and draw lines with an air-soluble pen 1 cm (½ in) and 2.2 cm (⅞ in) from the stitching and parallel to it (ii).

Iron folds along these lines. Fold the piping over the raw edge and topstitch along the line that forms at the bottom of the piping (iii). The edge should now be neatly finished (iv). Trim off any edges on the sides.

9. Fold the quilted piece of fabric so that the piped short edge is 17 cm (6¾ in) from the fold and pin it in position.

10. Neatly draw the corners of the flap using an air-soluble pen and a round object. Carefully cut the corners along these lines.

11. Stitch the entire case, except the bottom fold, with zigzag stitching.

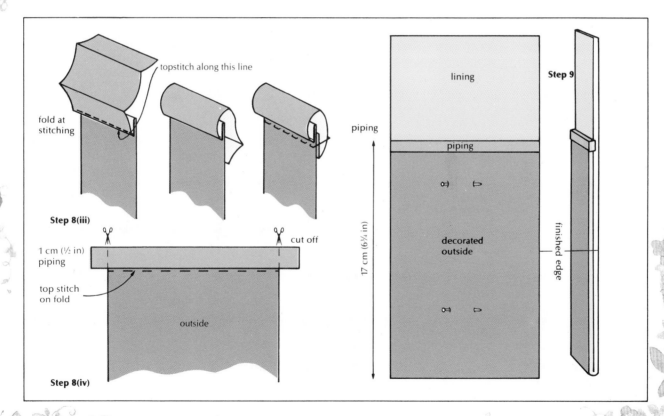

Step 10

Step 12, 13 and 14

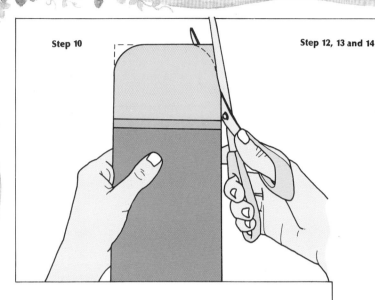

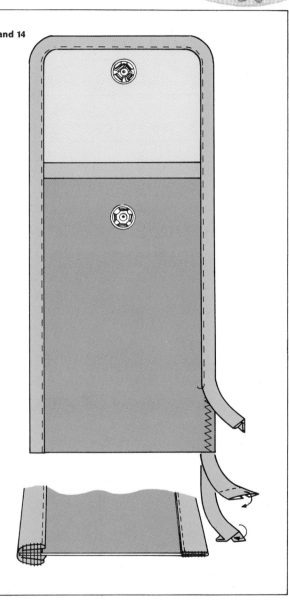

12. Iron the bias binding so that the pre-ironed edges are even and tack it to all the zigzagged edges. Neatly turn the bias binding in at the beginning and end. Work very precisely, or you might miss parts of the edges of the bias binding when stitching up the bag.

13. Stitch the bias binding with ordinary straight machine stitching. Zigzag stitching can be used, but the result is not as neat. Finish the beginning and end with slip-stitches.

14. Sew a press stud to the flap and in a corresponding position on the case to make a folded top.

HINT
To facilitate any sort of machine quilting, it is a good idea first to zigzag foam or polyester wadding together with the two pieces of fabric on either side of it around the entire outer edge. Bear in mind that if this is not done, the bottom fabric is inclined to crumple.

Envelope bags

A little quilted envelope bag has many uses and is a welcome gift, especially for a young girl. Made in pretty printed fabric, it can serve as a small handbag, pencil case, purse or even a make-up bag. Made in a plain neutral colour decorated with lace and ribbon or beads, it makes a beautiful evening bag. Finding pretty handbags for young girls is always a problem. Instead, make a small envelope bag, sew a long strap to it and you've got a bag that's both pretty and useful, and will be much appreciated.

Adapt the measurements given to suit yourself and give your imagination free rein. No two bags ever look alike, which is why it's such fun making them.

Requirements

1 thin layer of foam, 22 x 40 cm (8¾ x 16 in)
2 pieces plain preshrunk polycotton, approximately
*   22 x 40 cm (8¾ x 16 in) each*
1 piece broderie anglaise fabric, approximately 22 x 40 cm
*   (8¾ x 16 in), or strips of printed cotton fabric*
1 piece of cotton fabric, 22 x 40 cm (8¾ x 16 in) for the
*   lining*
80 cm (32 in) bias binding, 3.5 cm (1½ in) wide
A piece of fabric, approximately 3.5 x 24 cm (1½ x 9½ in)
*   for the piping — usually the same fabric as the lining*
An air-soluble pen
A press stud

Method

Also consult the diagrams under 'Glasses case'.

1. Cut out a rectangle 22 x 40 cm (8¾ x 16 in) from the foam — ensure that the corners are exactly square.
2. Using the foam as a pattern, cut out two pieces of cotton fabric. I usually use cream-coloured cotton sheeting which is inexpensive, easy to iron and goes with everything. Wash it before using it as some fabrics are inclined to shrink after the first wash or when steam-ironed. If you are making a broderie anglaise bag, cut out a third piece of material. Otherwise, the foam will show through the holes in the fabric when placed directly on top of the foam.
3. Pin the two pieces of fabric, one on each side of the foam with the right sides facing out. If you are using broderie anglaise, pin the broderie anglaise, one piece plain fabric, the foam and finally the second piece of plain fabric.
4. Zigzag all the layers around all four edges.
5. Decorate the bag according to your own taste. Use a thick needle (80-90) and fairly long stitches to complete this step.

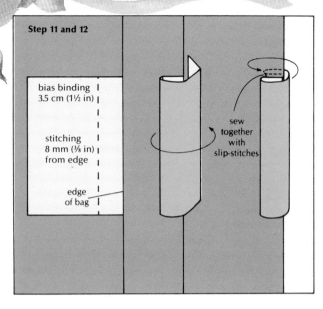

Lace and ribbon:
Using an air-soluble pen, draw guidelines and use them to sew on the decorations.

Strips of cotton print fabric:
Cut the fabric in strips according to taste. Then stitch the strips to the bag along the length or diagonally across the bag.

Sew strips on from left to right on the fabric and foam by positioning the first strip on the fabric and foam base with the right side facing up. The second strip of material is placed with the right side facing down on top of the first strip of fabric with its edge exactly even with the inside edge of the first strip of fabric. Stitch the two strips of material to the material and foam base, allowing 5 mm (¼ in) for the seam. Iron the seam open on the right side. Follow the same procedure with the 2nd and 3rd strips and all the following strips of fabric until the entire fabric and foam base is covered. Sew on any lace and ribbon trim.

6. Cut all the edges even with the finished zigzag edge of the material and foam base.
7. Pin the lining of the bag with the right side facing up to the back of the quilted and decorated material and foam base. Now pipe the upper front edge of the bag.
8. Place the 3.5 x 24 cm (1½ x 9½ in) piece of fabric on the outside of the bag and with the wrong side facing up and its edge even with the short edge of the bag that will be covered by the flap. Stitch, allowing 8 mm (⅜ in) for the seam. Fold the piece of material up and, using the air-soluble pen, draw lines parallel to the stitching 1 cm (½ in) and 2.2 cm (1 in) from the stitching. Iron folds along these lines. On the outside of the bag, stitch along the inside of the fold made between the small piece of fabric and the quilted piece of fabric. The edge is now neatly piped.
9. Fold the quilted fabric and foam so that the short edge is 14 cm (5½ in) from the fold and pin in the correct position.
10. Finish the corners of the flap neatly using an air-soluble pen and a round object. Neatly cut around the corners. You may find that the lining will come out slightly, but simply cut it even with the edge of the flap. Zigzag around the entire bag, except for the bottom fold.
11. Put the bag on a table with the outside of the flap facing upwards. Put the bias binding upside down on the bag with the one raw edge even with the edge of the bag and stitch 8 mm (⅜ in) from the edge. Take care not to stretch the bias binding at the corners or the flap will be crooked.
12. Fold the bias binding over the edge of the bag to form a piping and tack neatly. Carefully tuck the bias binding in at the ends. Sew the piping neatly to the other side with tiny slip-stitches.
13. Sew the press stud to the flap to keep it closed.
14. Make a satin bow and sew it to the outside of the bag with one or more bells. If you have any other trims, such as beads, embroidery, etc. they can be added at this stage.

Round potpourri bags

These bags make very useful gifts. They can be made from bits of leftover fabric and will delight anyone — young or old. Made to match the person's bedroom, it will be an even bigger surprise!

It's a good idea to have a few of these gifts handy. So while you're at it, you might as well make several and keep them until needed. They'll find homes in no time and soon you'll have to make another batch.

Requirements

2 pieces of fabric big enough to cut out circles with a 13 cm (5 in) diameter
1 piece of polyester wadding, 10 x 10 x 1 cm (4 x 4 x ½ in)
Lace and ribbon for decoration
Approximately 50 ml (4 tbl) potpourri (see recipe on page 18)
A piece of cotton wool
A few drops of essential oil

Method

1. Cut out two fabric circles, each 13 cm (5 in) in diameter. I use a saucer and draw the outline with a pencil or an air-soluble pen — it's much easier than using a compass.

2. Fold one fabric circle in half to determine the centre line. Sew lace and ribbon symmetrically along each side of this centre line or work decorative stitching. The decoration should be 6-8 cm (2½-3 in) wide.

3. Cut out one circle 10 cm (4 in) in diameter from polyester wadding. Divide it in two layers.

4. Sandwich the layers of the bag as follows: put the undecorated fabric circle flat with the wrong side facing upwards and place the first layer of wadding on top. Put the potpourri and a piece of cotton wool with a few drops of essential oil on the wadding. The cotton wool absorbs the oil which would otherwise seep through on to the fabric, leaving ugly grease marks. Next, put the second layer of wadding on top of the bottom layer, and

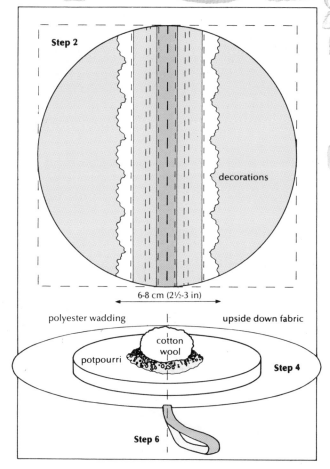

finally the second, decorated piece of material with the right side up.

5. Pin the pieces of fabric, with the wadding and potpourri sandwiched between them, neatly together.

6. Fold an 18-cm (7-in) length of narrow ribbon in half and insert the raw edges between the two pieces of fabric, directly opposite the centre line, to form a loop for hanging up the bag.

7. Sew up the bag by zigzagging or overcasting all along the edge of the outer two pieces of fabric.

8. Approximately 5 mm (¼ in) from the edge of the bag, sew the gathered lace to the decorated side of the bag, as follows: Start stitching at the top near the loop, approximately 1 cm (½ in) from the one end of the lace. Stitch all the way around, stopping approximately 1 cm (½ in) from the beginning. Cut the lace, allowing 2 cm (1 in) more than the circumference of the bag. Tuck in the ends and finish the stitching.

9. Tie off all the loose threads and wrap the bag in a plastic sandwich bag to keep the scent in until the bag is to be used.

A cover for any basket

Baskets come in a wide variety of shapes and size. Covered, they are even more attractive and useful.

Because baskets are made by hand, no two baskets have the exact same measurements. Read the instructions carefully before buying material, lace and ribbon for a cover. I've used a rectangular basket as an example, but a cover for any round or oval basket is made in exactly the same way.

Requirements

Cotton print or plain cotton fabric
Satin ribbon, 8 mm (⅜ in) and 25 mm (1 in) wide
Broderie anglaise lace
A piece of thin foam or polyester wadding
Elastic, 5 mm (¼ in) wide
An air-soluble pen

Method

1. Cut out a piece of paper exactly the same size as the base of the basket.

2. Using this paper pattern, determine the circumference of the base of the basket.

3. Measure the depth of the basket on the inside and also decide how far you would like the cover to come over the edge of the basket. An unattractive basket can be cleverly hidden under a wide cover, but most baskets are so pretty that one wants to show off some of the basketwork.

4. Using the measurements in 2 and 3 above, calculate how much material, lace and ribbon is required.

Cotton fabric is usually 90 cm (36 in) wide. For example, if the measurements of the basket are as follows:

Base: 20 x 30 cm (8 x 12 in), circumference = 100 cm (40 in)

Depth and overlap + seam at the base = 28 cm (11 in) For a basket that is not wider at the top, you require fabric approximately 1½ to 2 times the circumference of the base of the basket.

For a basket that is wider at the top than the bottom, you require fabric approximately 1¾ to 2¼ times the circumference of the base of the basket.

The basket in the example is slightly wider at the top than the bottom, so two entire widths of fabric are required. The selvedges trimmed off are 90 cm − 2 cm = 88 cm (36 in − 1 in = 35 in).

The amount of material required is thus as follows: 2 x 28 cm (11 in) + 20 cm (8 in) (width of the base) = approximately 80 cm (30 in)

Amount of lace required:
Circumference of the cover = 2 x 113 cm (44 in)
 Approximately 230 cm (88 in) = 2.3 m (2½ yd)

Amount of narrow lace required:
Circumference of the cover + ribbons on both sides of the seams at the handle + ribbon for sewing on the hearts = 2 x 113 cm (44 in) + 4 x 28 cm (11 in) + 2 x 20 cm (8 in)
 Approximately 380 cm (126 in) = 3.8 m (3½ yd)

Amount of wide ribbon required:
Approximately 2.5 m (2½ yd) per basket if you wish to decorate the handle.

Amount of elastic required:
Approximately the circumference of the base, ie 1.1 m (1¼ yd).

5. Cut off two 28 cm (11 in) widths of fabric. Trim the selvedges and pin the short edges together, ensuring that the design on the fabric runs in the same direction. Place the two seams opposite the handle of the basket. If your basket has two handles, make two extra seams. Measure how far the seams should be stitched up to allow the loose ends to cover both ends of the handle.
6. Stitch 1.5 cm (⅝ in) wide seams as far as the given points. Zigzag the edges of the seams.
7. Iron the seams open as though the stitching runs all the way.
8. This step is optional, but will give the cover a more attractive appearance: on the right side, stitch a narrow ribbon on each side of the fold of the seam and its extension. Ensure, however, that the seam is out of the way at the back and that you stitch only through a single layer of material.
9. Zigzag each of the two long sides of the cover.
10. One edge of broderie anglaise is usually left raw and cut in a scalloped form. Straighten this edge and zigzag it neatly and thoroughly. Draw a line 8 mm (⅜ in) from, and parallel to this edge, across the entire length

of the lace using an air-soluble pen. Cut the lace into two equal pieces.
11. Place the fabric on the lace in such a way that the zigzagged edge of the cotton print is in line with the line you have drawn on the right side of the lace, and sew the cotton print to the lace.

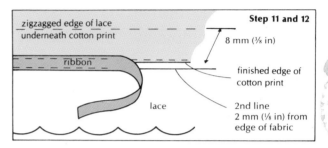

12. Draw a second line on the lace 2 mm (⅛ in) from the edge of the fabric using the air-soluble pen. With one edge of the narrow ribbon even with this line and the other edge on the cotton print, stitch along both edges of the ribbon.
13. Zigzag the raw edges of the lace and ribbon at the seam and fold back 1.5 cm (⅝ in).
14. Divide the other raw edge of the cover in four equal sections, using the seams as two of the dividing points. Place them on top of one another and use the folds in the fabric as the other two dividing points. Mark these points clearly with the air-soluble pen. Stitch a double tacking thread along this edge of the cover.
15. Using the paper pattern of the base of the basket, cut out a piece of foam and two pieces of fabric. With the right sides of the fabric facing out, zigzag the fabric and the foam together all the way around.
16. Machine quilt the fabric and foam. Decide on a pattern such as diagonal or vertical lines, diamonds or squares, and draw the guidelines on the material using a ruler and the air-soluble pen. Using a thick needle (80-90), quilt the material. Ensure that every starting

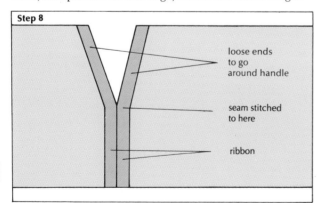

and finishing point is well finished to prevent it from coming undone.

17. Mark the midpoint of each side of the base section of the cover.

18. Evenly draw in the tacking on the basket cover and place the seams on the midpoints of the long sides of the base and the other dividing points on the centre point of the short sides of the base. Ensure that the right sides of the fabric face each other. Make sure that the raw edge of the cover is exactly in line with the finished edge of the base section.

19. Carefully stitch the drawn-in basket cover to the base section, approximately 5 mm (¼ in) from the raw edge. Then zigzag the raw edge and edge of the base together.

20. Put the cover in the basket and determine where the elastic should be sewn on.

21. At this point, draw a line on the wrong side of the fabric parallel to the finished edge of the lace. In the example the distance is 2 cm (1 in).

22. Take a sufficient length of elastic for the cover to fit snugly around the basket — approximately two thirds of the circumference of the basket — and divide it in two. Then divide each section into four and mark these points. Also divide the stitching guideline into four by carefully folding the fabric in half and then in half again.

23: Pin the elastic's dividing points to the corresponding dividing points on the wrong side of the fabric. Zigzag the elastic to the cover. Using your left hand, stretch the elastic and hold it in position while stitching. If you find this awkward, divide both the elastic and guideline in eighths and pin the elastic at shorter distances.

24. Next, fit the cover over the basket, ensuring that the seams have not been stitched up too far. If you find that this is the case, unpick the seams a short way.

25. Wrap the wide ribbon around the handle and cut it at the required point. Seal the loose ends, tuck them underneath the cover and sew firmly to the cover by hand. Also firmly sew the two loose ends covering the handle to the elastic.

26. Cut the rest of the wide ribbon in two and tie bows to the handle.

27. Make four sweet-smelling hearts (see p. 33 for instructions) and sew two to each end of a 20-cm (8-in) length of narrow ribbon. Hang them around the handle and sew the ribbon and bows to the cover, ensuring that both the hearts and the bows are very secure.

HINT

Any worn-out basket can be revived by soaking it in water to remove all the dust and then drying it. Spray two layers of varnish over the entire basket once it has dried.

Appliqué to decorate your home

The art of appliqué offers endless possibilities. The three examples discussed here will hopefully inspire you to do your own creative designs. Always keep your eyes open for pretty pieces of fabric and attractive designs to use for your own original appliqué pictures.

INSTRUCTIONS FOR APPLIQUÉ

Requirements
Pencil and paper
Tracing paper
A very sharp pair scissors with sharp points
Thin iron-on bonding fabric (glued on one side only)
A glue stick
An air-soluble pen
Thread with a sheen
Fabric
Embroidery or picture frame

Method

1. Always choose a simple design. More detail can be added by doing machine stitching and embroidery or by sewing on beads and other decorations later.

2. Draw the actual size of the design on paper.

3. Separately number and trace each section of the design on a sheet of tracing paper. Allow for overlapping sections of the fabric by adding 5 mm (¼ in) to the bottom layer of fabric. The walls of a house, overlapped by the roof, is a typical example. To determine the actual size of a design that is to be framed, add 5 mm (¼ in) all the way around to the inside circumference of the frame.

4. Cut out each section neatly.

5. Choose different fabrics for each section of the design – remember, contrast is vital. Always use non-stretch fabric and preferably natural fibres like cotton or linen. A piece of satin livens up any design.

6. Trace the circumference of the frame on the background fabric and cut out the material, adding 3 cm (1⅛ in) all the way around.

7. Using a piece of fabric slightly larger than each of the patterns, iron the glued side of the thin bonding fabric to the back of the fabric. Use an ordinary dry iron – a steam iron will cause the bonding fabric to crumple.

8. Pin the paper patterns to the pieces of fabric with the ironed on bonding, and neatly and accurately cut out each pattern piece. Number each small piece of fabric with the air-soluble pen so that you can identify each one.

9. Arrange the design exactly on the background material and mark the exact position of the small pieces of fabric using an air-soluble pen, as the marks will eventually disappear.

10. Remove the small pieces of fabric and, one by one, glue them to the background fabric starting from the background and working to the foreground. Ensure that all the edges are glued down well. Remember, if one piece of fabric is to be overlapped by another, glue the former down first.

11. Stitch the pieces of fabric around the edges with closely-worked satin stitch. Before working on the actual item, experiment on another piece of fabric to ensure that the stitch width and density is correct. Also ensure that the bottom thread does not show through on the top. You may find that sometimes it is necessary to tighten the tension of the bottom thread or, in the case of some machines, the thread can be inserted through a hole in the bobbin, as when making buttonholes.

12. Make sure you always work clockwise, ensuring that the needle is just slightly off the edge of the piece of fabric that is being appliquéd when it is on the righthand side. Try working evenly around corners without stopping. At a sharp corner or when you do need to stop, ensure that the needle is always on the inside (left) of the piece of fabric and that it remains inserted in the fabric as you lift the foot. Then turn the work before you continue to stitch.

13. The different sections of the design are stitched on in the same sequence as the one used when they were glued to the background fabric, ie from the background to the foreground.

14. To finish off the threads, thread them to the back, knot and cut them 3 mm (⅛ in) from the knot. Seal them with a little glue to ensure they don't come undone.

15. After all the pieces of fabric have been sewn on, do any additional decorative machine sewing.

16. Iron the work very thoroughly.

17. Do any last-minute hand decoration at this stage.

18. Frame or mount the appliqué.

HINTS

☐ *Colouring books often have attractive designs for appliqué.*

☐ *Use French knots (see page 55) to round off any needlework.*

Hearts and doves for a little girl

This beautiful decoration for a girl's bedroom can be made in no time. Make a few at a time, varying the pieces of fabric (see photograph on page 24) so that each one is unique.

Requirements

See the instructions for appliqué on page 46 and the pattern on page 86
7 different toning pieces of fabric
1.5 m (1⅝ yd) satin ribbon, 1 cm (½ in) wide
An embroidery hoop, approximately 20 cm (8 in) in diameter on the inside
Embroidery thread for French knots to make the central heart and the doves' eyes
Liquid glue
A 22 x 22-cm (9 x 9-in) square of felt

Method

1. Follow the instructions for appliqué. Glue, but do not stitch the central heart.
2. Mount the appliqué in the embroidery frame so that the design is in the centre of the frame. Tighten the screw, which should be at the centre top, and stretch the appliqué very tight in the frame.
3. Cut the background fabric at the back of the frame, leaving a 1-cm (½-in) edge.
4. Apply glue thickly to the back of the inside ring of the hoop, fold the edge to the inside and press it to the glued edge with your fingers. The fabric should be saturated with glue. At first it might seem as though the fabric won't stick. Leave it a while for the glue to become tacky. Press the fabric down again and repeat until it lies flat on the surface of the wood. Leave the glue to dry thoroughly.
5. Using very sharp scissors, cut the remainder of the background fabric even with the edge of the hoop. ·
6. Using four strands of embroidery thread in a contrasting colour, embroider knots (see page 55) around the heart in the centre of the hoop. Make each knot right next to the heart and as close to the next

one as possible. Or work machine satin stitch as shown in the photograph.
7. Make three French knots for the doves' eyes.
8. Put glue on a piece of paper and leave a little while to become tacky.
9. Measure a piece of ribbon to cover the outer edge of the hoop and seal the ends.
10. Apply the tacky glue to the outer edge of the embroidery hoop. Do not use too much glue or it could leave grease marks on the ribbon.
11. Glue the ribbon to the edge of the hoop with the one edge of the ribbon exactly in line with the front edge of the embroidery frame. Leave the glue to dry.
12. Fold the remaining ribbon in half and make a knot

21.5 cm (8½ in) from the fold to make a loop from which to hang the frame.

13. Insert the loose ends of the ribbon from behind through the opening below the screw of the frame. Bring the loose ends to the front, one on either side of the screw, and make a pretty bow. Cut the ends of the ribbon at an angle and seal them.

14. Cut a felt circle slightly smaller than the outer edge of the embroidery frame and glue it to the back edge of the frame to finish the decoration at the back.

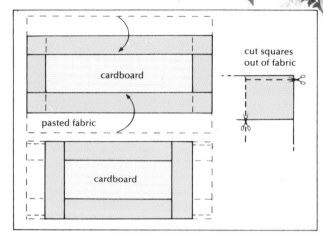

> **HINT**
> *The gift can be made extra special by inserting a potpourri bag between the picture and the felt backing.*

Pictures in fabric

An appliquéd picture framed in a ready-made frame is a gift that will enhance any home. We have given two examples of each of these pictures. Once you have completed them, you will probably have many ideas of your own.

Requirements

See the instructions for appliqué and the patterns on pages 88 and 89
Background fabric measuring 17.5 x 22.5 cm (7 x 9 in)
9 different toning pieces of fabric
2 standard 127 x 178 mm (5 x 7 in) wooden frames with glass
Liquid glue
2 pieces of stiff cardboard, 12.5 x 17.5 cm (5 x 7 in) each
Brown paper for finishing the frames at the back

Method

1. Follow the instructions for working appliqué on page 46.

2. Position the frame without its glass on top of the completed appliqué and trace the inside circumference of the frame with an air-soluble pen.

3. Stitch 2 mm (⅛ in) on the outside of this mark all the way around the appliqué.

4. Put the appliqué, with the right side facing down, on a table and position the cardboard on top. Glue the cardboard and leave for a while to allow the glue to become tacky. Glue the two long sides of the appliqué to it. Ensure that the appliqué is tightly stretched and keep it in position by inserting pins at right angles in the cardboard. Leave the glue to dry thoroughly.

5. Cut squares from the corners of the background fabric as shown above and glue the other two opposite sides of the appliqué as described in 4 above.

6. Insert the clean glass and picture in the frame and secure them.

7. Neatly glue brown paper to the back of the picture and frame to finish.

The patterns for the two top pictures appear on page 88 and 89, the bottom pictures are variations of these.

CHAPTER 4

Gifts in cross stitch

Once you start doing cross stitch, you can become hooked for life. Apparently, it is not only women who enjoy it as a pastime. I recently read a letter in an American cross stitch magazine from a woman who writes that she and her husband do cross stitch work every day of their lives.

Cross stitch has many advantages in addition to being great fun. You can do it anywhere; if it's a small item you can easily fit it into your bag and work while waiting for an appointment at the doctor or even while travelling by plane. In no time you will have made many beautiful little gifts.

You can, however, also make large heirlooms. There are numerous cross stitch pieces in museums around the world that date back many centuries.

51

INSTRUCTIONS FOR ITEMS IN CROSS STITCH

1. Cut the fabric to the required size and immediately zigzag the raw edges on your sewing machine. The fabric frays easily and your piece of fabric can soon become smaller and smaller.

2. Lightly fold the fabric in half to determine the midpoint on the sides. Using a piece of bright cotton thread (ordinary sewing thread will do), tack a guideline from the middle of one side to the middle of the opposite side. Tack each stitch over four threads of the fabric. Tack the second guideline perpendicular to the first, but sew from the centre of the piece of fabric to ensure that the lines cross at the same point. This centre point is usually indicated on any cross stitch chart or pattern.

3. With this centre point in the middle, firmly stretch the piece of fabric over an embroidery frame.

4. Always use two strands of embroidery thread, unless instructed otherwise. If the fabric is very coarse, you will need to use more threads. If you separate each strand singly and then pair them up, the thread is less likely to twist on the needle.

5. Start by determining the exact position of the design on the piece of fabric. Each square on the charts given in this book represents two threads on the fabric. Insert the needle from the top to the bottom near this position, bringing it to the top in the bottom left-hand corner of the square. Insert it downwards in the top right-hand corner of the square.

Finish a row and return in the opposite direction to complete the crosses. Note: you should ensure that the bottom stitches of the crosses all lie in the same direction, and that the top stitches all lie in the opposite direction. Remember, with cross stitch, most of the threads at the back should lie vertically from the top to the bottom.

6. The term back stitch is often used in cross stitch patterns. This is done once the crosses have been

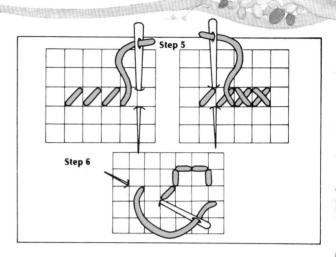

completed in order to outline and finish the work. On patterns given in this book, work back stitch vertically, horizontally or diagonally across two threads on the right side of the fabric, and across four threads on the wrong side of the fabric.

7. Complete a section before tying off the threads. Do not use the same threads at the back to continue with the next design as it will show through on the front.

8. Once the work has been completed, iron the back using a very hot iron and damp (not wet) cloth. Do not iron the front as the thread will lose its sheen.

9. Roll up the piece of fabric or keep it flat until it is to be used or framed – do not fold it.

10. Framed needlework does not usually need mounting. If you are in any doubt, take your work to a specialist in framing needlework. Some designs look beautiful when lined simply at the back, but remember, dust can be a problem and once an item has been washed it is never the same again. If you are making an heirloom, it is worth spending the extra money to have it framed. Alternatively, the work should be rolled up and wrapped in acid-free tissue paper.

BUILDING UP A LIBRARY OF EMBROIDERY THREADS

Embroidery thread is not cheap and can cost a small fortune. Certain colours are very popular and are used again and again in different patterns. Unless you keep track you could end up buying the same colour more than once without realizing it. To prevent this from happening and also to get the maximum use from your thread, you should build up a library of embroidery threads. Cut the threads in easily manageable lengths before use and keep them with their corresponding number — this will forever solve the problem of not knowing colour numbers.

Cut out a 5 x 15 cm (2 x 6 in) piece of cardboard or heavy paper. Punch holes 1.5 cm (¾ in) apart along one of the long sides. Take a piece of thread and write its number next to the hole. Unravel the entire hank and fold it into convenient lengths of approximately 45 cm (18 in). Cut both ends, insert them through the hole with the appropriate number and thread them into a loop.

Kept neatly together like this in a tin or box, your embroidery threads will never again become knotted into useless bunches.

It is also useful to keep a notebook in which you can record the numbers you already have. Arrange them numerically. Also indicate when you have run out of a certain number thread to facilitate checking what you have in stock. Buy sufficient thread to finish an entire item, as colours vary with each batch.

813

742

666

HINTS
□ *If the available fabric has a finer or coarser weave than is indicated in the pattern, compensate for this when cutting the fabric. You will need less fabric if the weave is finer, and more if it is coarser.*
□ *Any design that can be drawn on graph paper can be done in cross stitch.*
□ *Write your own name, your relationship to the recipient and the date at the back of any framed item in cross stitch. Human beings are curious by nature and will want to know its origin.*

Hearts in crosses

This design is good for beginners and makes pretty lavender bags to give as gifts.

Requirements
*4 pieces of evenweave fabric, 9 x 12 cm (3½ x 4¾ in),
    12 threads/cm (24 threads/in)
An embroidery frame, 16 cm (6 in) in diameter
A tapestry needle
1 m (1 yd) of ribbon, 4 mm (3/16 in) wide
An air-soluble pen
Dry lavender flowers with which to fill the bags
Gold bells for decoration
Gold embroidery thread
Stranded embroidery thread in three successive colours*

Note: See p. 90 for the pattern and suggested colours

Method
1. Follow the instructions for items in cross stitch.
2. With the air-soluble pen, draw lines on the wrong side of the embroidery, 22 threads from the last cross stitch on the sides and 14 threads from the bottom.
3. With right sides of the embroidery and the plain fabric together, stitch along the guidelines to form a bag. Trim the seams to a width of 5 mm (¼ in) and finish the open seams in zigzag. Turn the bags inside out.
4. Mark the bag 17.5 cm (7 in) from the bottom seam and fold a double seam 10 threads wide to the inside. Using the lightest of the three threads, and tacking stitches, sew a seam 8 threads from the fold across two threads of the fabric. When you have worked around once, sew a second row of stitches to fill the gaps in the previous row to ensure that the seam is neat inside as well as outside.
5. Fill with lavender flowers, tie with a satin ribbon and decorate with bells.

Chefs for the kitchen

This picture of chefs in cross stitch makes a very original gift. The pattern is easy enough for a beginner to master it.

Requirements
*20 x 35 cm (8 x 14 in) evenweave fabric, 24 threads/in, in
    écru
An embroidery frame, 16 cm (6 in) in diameter
A tapestry needle
Stranded embroidery thread*

Note: See p. 90 for the pattern and suggested colours.

Method
1. Follow the instructions for items in cross stitch.

Home, Sweet Home

This sampler makes a special gift for a friend or relation who is moving into a new house.

Requirements
*20 x 30 cm (8 x 12 in) evenweave fabric, 12 threads/cm
    (24 threads/in)
An embroidery frame, 16 cm (6 in) in diameter
A tapestry needle
Stranded embroidery thread*

Note: See p. 91 for the pattern and suggested colours

Method
1. Follow the instructions for items in cross stitch.
2. Using 4 strands of thread, work the French knots when the rest of the embroidery has been completed. (See opposite.)

FRENCH KNOTS

1. Pull the needle up through the fabric at a. Twist the thread being held between thumb and forefinger of the left hand around the front of the needle, which should be held upright, to the right, and left around the back. Hold the needle and thread with the thumb and forefinger of the right hand.

2. Lower the needle from the upright position to a more horizontal position and pull the thread tight around the needle.

3. Once more, twist the thread to the front over the needle to the right, and underneath to the left. From above it will look like a figure of eight.

4. Pull the thread tight with the left hand and raise the needle to an upright position. Insert the needle at b directly next to the spot where it came through from the bottom at a, push it through the fabric and pull the needle and thread clear towards the back.

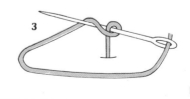

Hummel characters in cross stitch

The 'Singing Quartet' is another lovely little heirloom based on the charming and original drawing of a Franciscan nun, Sister Maria Innocentia Hummel.

Berta Hummel — her secular name — was born on 21 May 1909 in Massing near Munich. She grew up with her five sisters in a house where music, art and religion were a way of life. Even as a little girl she enjoyed drawing and painting the familiar objects in her world, such as flowers, birds, small animals, and her school friends.

After finishing school, she enrolled at the Munich Acadamy for Fine Art in 1927. Two of her fellow students were Franciscan nuns. She also decided to become a nun and on 30 August 1934 she took her vows. In the Siessen convent near Saulgau (Württemberg), the now-consecrated Sister Maria Innocentia, inspired by all her beautiful memories, began sketching her friends who had made her childhood 'heaven on earth'.

These drawings soon became well known and very popular. The W. Goebel factory, famed for its porcelain and ceramics, approached the Siessen convent to obtain world rights to turn the sketches into three-dimensional *objets d'art*. Under the loving but strict supervision of the artist, the first Hummel characters were produced a year later. These characters became so popular that soon they were dubbed 'the world's favourite children'.

The war and the difficult years that followed proved too much for Sister Maria Innocentia and she died on 6 November 1946.

Requirements

20 x 30 cm (8 x 12 in) evenweave fabric, 12 threads/cm (24 threads/in)
An embroidery frame, 16 cm (6 in) in diameter
A tapestry needle
Stranded embroidery thread

Note: See p. 92 for the pattern and suggested colours

Method

1. Follow the instructions for items in cross stitch. To give the eyes of the two boys in the foreground a round appearance, make an X stitch and a + stitch to make a *.

A wedding sampler for newly-weds

A wedding day is very special, and therefore deserves a very special gift. Make this sampler for someone who is very close to you — your children — or perhaps for your own wedding.

Requirements

30 x 40 cm (8 x 12 in) evenweave fabric, 12 threads/cm (24 threads/in)
Embroidery frame, 16 cm (6 in) in diameter
A tapestry needle
Stranded embroidery cotton

Note: See p. 93 for the pattern and suggested colours

Method

1. Follow the instructions for items in cross stitch.

HINT
Cross stitch designs can be embroidered on any ordinary piece of fabric. Begin by tacking a piece of Hardanger canvas, or any other evenly woven fabric, to the item to be worked. The evenweave fabric must be slightly bigger than the design to be embroidered. Work the design as usual, using the evenweave cloth as a guide. Ensure that the stitches are pulled tight. Cut the embroidery cloth close to the embroidered design and, one by one, remove the threads of the embroidery cloth underneath the design.

CHAPTER 5
Painted gifts

*Armed with a paintbrush and poster paint, and
with a little bit of time and patience, you can make
unusual gifts using brown medicine bottles and
ready-made, unpainted wooden picture frames.
It might take a bit of practice at first to perfect the
flowers, but once you've mastered the knack, it's
really quick and easy to do.
It is also very easy to let your own creativity come to
the fore. Use the ideas in this chapter as a basis, and
decorate all kinds of objects, such as storage canisters and
jars, or even mirrors with dull wooden frames.
It is always a source of wonder to see how even
the most uninteresting and mundane object can, with
a little attention, be transformed from something you
would rather throw away into something you would
want to display with pride and pleasure.*

59

INSTRUCTIONS FOR PAINTING THE FLOWERS

Requirements

A very fine paintbrush
Gold poster paint
Dark blue, dark red or maroon poster paint
Off-white poster paint

Method

1. Ensure that the surface on which you want to paint the flowers is clean and dry.
2. Shake the paint well.
3. Always use the gold paint first and cover the surface you wish to decorate with small and large flowers, each with four petals and lots of small dots in between. Leave the paint to dry thoroughly before applying the next colour.
4. Use one of the other two colour paints — usually the dark colour — and paint a small petal on each of the larger gold petals. Also paint smaller coloured flowers between the other flowers. Leave the paint to dry thoroughly.
5. Use the off-white paint or mix it with the coloured paint to obtain a lighter colour, and paint a dot in the centre of each large flower, as well as lots of smaller flowers and dots in between the completed flowers. Always leave the paint to dry thoroughly after each step and before using the article.

HINTS

☐ *Make your own unique writing paper using plain writing or typing paper. Paint a few of these flowers in one or more of the corners of the paper. If it is for someone very special, you can also paint a few hearts in gold in between the flowers.*
☐ *Give the paper a wonderful aroma by putting a drop of essential oil on a piece of cardboard. Cover this piece of cardboard with another piece of cardboard and place it in the bottom of the container for your writing paper. The extra piece of cardboard will prevent the oil from making grease marks on the paper.*

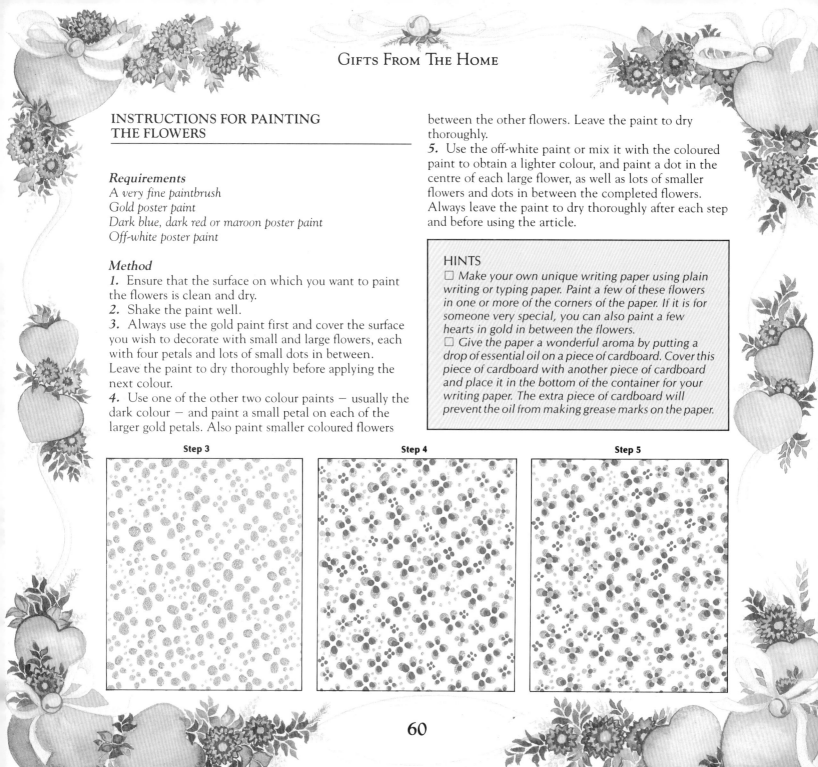

Step 3

Step 4

Step 5

Medicine bottles decorated with flowers

Who would ever have thought that ordinary brown medicine bottles could look this beautiful? Make them in sets of three to enhance any corner of your home.

Requirements
Brown medicine bottles with cork or screw-on tops
A very fine paintbrush
Gold poster paint
Dark blue, dark red or maroon poster paint
Off-white poster paint
Indoor wood sealer (glossy)
Lace, ribbon and fabric for the covers
Thin round elastic
Approximately 30 cm (12 in) satin ribbon for each bottle

Method
1. Follow the instructions for painting the flowers.
2. Seal the paint work by painting a layer of wood sealer over it. Ordinary varnish is inclined to change the colour of the paint.
3. Make covers for the bottles (see page 27).

New frames for old photographs

Family photographs have once again become very popular home decorations. Many photographs, however, remain packed away because they aren't framed. Attractive frames are very expensive, while cheaper ones unfortunately look exactly that. Here is a perfect solution – frames that are both attractive and affordable! Here are two possibilities – both equally pretty and easy to make.

Brown wooden frames with decorated mountings

Requirements

A ready-made, unpainted wooden frame with a flat ledge on the inside for the gold paint
A 1-1.5 cm (½-¾ in) wide paintbrush
Wood stain (medium oak)
Indoor wood sealer (glossy)
A very fine paintbrush
Gold poster paint
Dark blue, dark red or maroon poster paint
Off-white poster paint
Dark blue mounting board
A craft knife and ruler
Masking tape and brown paper

Method

1. Finish the frame with wire wool if necessary.
2. Stain the wood by applying the stain with a paintbrush. Leave it to dry thoroughly. The number of layers will depend on your taste.
3. Carefully paint the vertical edge and the flat ledge on the inside of the frame with undiluted gold poster paint. Leave the paint to dry thoroughly.
4. Seal the wood by applying the sealer with a paintbrush. Two coats are usually required.
5. Cut the mounting board to the required size with the craft knife and ruler.

6. Draw the correct position of the oval (see page 94 for ovals of various sizes) for the photograph on the board with a pencil. Carefully cut out the opening with the craft knife.
7. Paint the vertical edge of the oval in the mounting board, and approximately 2 mm (⅛ in) around the outer edge of the oval with undiluted gold poster paint. The line around the opening need not be completely even.
8. Paint flowers around the outside of the oval according to the instructions. Use mostly gold paint and only touches of coloured paint. You can also change the position of the light and dark paints as specified in the instructions.

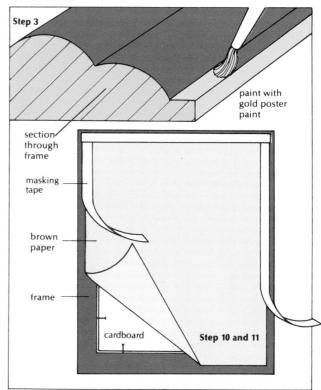

Step 3

paint with gold poster paint

section through frame

masking tape

brown paper

frame

cardboard

Step 10 and 11

9. Mount the photograph by securing it in the correct position at the back of the mounting board with masking tape.

10. Put the clean glass, mounted photograph and the piece of cardboard that comes with the frame back into the frame. Bend the wire loops, clamps or nails back to firmly secure the mounting.

11. Cover the back of the frame with brown paper and seal it with masking tape.

Painted frames decorated with flowers

Requirements

A ready-made, unpainted wooden frame with a rebate on the inside for the gold paint
PVA paint for painting the frame — pink, blue or maroon
A 1-1.5 cm (½-¾ in) wide paintbrush
A very fine paintbrush
Gold poster paint
Dark blue, red or maroon poster paint
Off-white poster paint
Indoor wood sealer (glossy)
Multi-purpose adhesive glue
Mounting board
Lace
A craft knife and ruler
Masking tape and brown paper

Method

1. Finish the frame with wire wool if necessary.

2. Paint the frame with PVA paint in the required background colour and leave to dry thoroughly. Two layers are usually sufficient.

3. Very carefully paint the vertical edge and flat ledge on the inside of the frame with undiluted gold poster paint. Leave the paint to dry thoroughly.

4. Paint the flowers on the frame as shown on page 60. I usually paint flowers in the corners only, but use your own discretion. Leave to dry.

5. Seal the flowers by painting on wood sealer.

6. Cut the mounting board to the required size with the craft knife and ruler.

7. Draw the correct position of the oval area (see page 94) for the photograph on the board with a pencil. Carefully cut out the opening with the craft knife.

8. Paint the vertical edge of the oval in the mounting board, and approximately 2 mm (⅛ in) around the outer edge of the oval with undiluted gold poster paint. The line around the opening need not be absolutely even.

9. Mark the position for glueing the lace to the mounting board. In the photograph on page 63, the lace is just on the inside of the frame, while on page 65 the lace has been glued on the mount as an 'inner' frame.

10. Cut the lace so that the ends overlap at the corners.

11. Remove the lace from the mounting, and place it with the right side facing down on a clean sheet of white paper. Spray the lace with glue.

12. Secure the lace to the mounting and cut the corners at a 45° angle so that the pieces fit exactly.

13. You could even glue a satin bow or two to the mounting if you like.

14. Mount the photograph by securing it in the correct position at the back of the mounting board with masking tape.

15. When all this is done, put the clean glass, mounted photograph and piece of cardboard that comes with the frame back into the frame. You should bend the wire loops, clamps or nails back to firmly secure the mounting.

16. Seal the back of the frame with strips of masking tape around the entire frame and the adjoining cardboard.

HINTS

☐ These frames look attractive hung up on a satin ribbon and brass ring. Cut a 10 cm (4 in) length of satin ribbon, 1-2 cm (½-1 in) wide, and thread it through a brass ring. Fold the satin ribbon in half with the raw edges overlapping. Secure the ribbon to the centre top back of the frame with a small nail, or staple it. Hang it on the ring as is. If you wish, glue a satin bow to the ribbon just below the brass ring from which the portrait is hanging.

☐ The mounting can be made even more interesting by spraying the wrong side of pretty floral or striped fabric with spray glue and glueing the fabric to the pre-cut mounting board. Cut out an opening in the centre of the fabric through the opening in the board. The opening in the fabric must, however, be 1.5 cm (¾ in) larger all around than the opening in the board. Cut notches in this 1.5 cm (¾ in) overlap and fold it over the opening. Glue it to the back of the mounting board. It takes a bit of practice to glue the fabric so that it is flat and has no air bubbles, but once you've mastered the technique, you can cover books, files and boxes in this way.

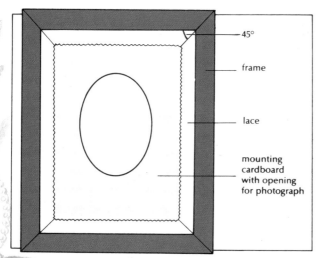

45°

frame

lace

mounting cardboard with opening for photograph

As a variation, paste the photographs directly onto the mounting, draw gold lines with a pen, and finish with lace.

CHAPTER 6

Gifts the whole family can make

Families can do much to strengthen their ties by making gifts together. It's great fun pottering in the garage or family room to produce something tangible to give to others. One can also use this time to teach children basic handicraft skills and to instil in them a love of working with their hands, an ability which will stand them in good stead later in life. Thousands of people can vouch for the fact that an interest in hobbies and handicrafts enriches one's life forever.

Turn the making of gifts into a special event by involving the children and giving them plenty of opportunity to experiment. Parents can do the more difficult tasks in the beginning and the children the easier ones. They will soon be able to initiate and complete their own projects.

67

Herb posies

These original and easy-to-make gifts go down well with everyone. They are made from bits of leftover cotton fabric, and everyday herbs and spices that are used in the kitchen. If you have a lavender or rosemary bush in your garden, you can dry some of the flowers and leaves for this purpose.

The kids will also enjoy giving you a hand while you're making the posies; in fact, the entire family can join in the fun while watching television. Make a few at a time, because this is the type of gift that is perfect for any occasion. At Christmas time, for example, you can make gifts as well as decorations using red, green and white pieces of fabric and ribbons.

Sort out your leftover bits of fabric and put all the cotton and polycotton oddments in a bag. Before long, you can use up all those leftovers to make gifts that will provide someone else with great pleasure. Although you might have to buy a small piece of fabric now and then, this is still a clever way of using up oddments creatively.

The doilies are available from most supermarkets and stationery departments. Or, if you have a lot of extra energy, you can make your own using cardboard, fabric and lace. Some doilies are printed on net and sealed in plastic. They look most effective if the edges are cut out with a small pair of scissors. It only takes a few minutes, but the end result is much prettier.

Depending on the size of the doily, you have to decide whether you want to make large or small balls. Whatever the case, it's important that the posy does not end up looking sparse.

Requirements

11 oddments of cotton fabric in three or four different toning colours or shades. Ideally, there should be at least two or three bits of cloth in the same plain colour. Use 7.5 x 7.5 cm (3 x 3 in) pieces of fabric for the small posies and 10 x 10 cm (4 x 4 in) for the bigger ones.

Approximately 20 pieces of very fine florist's wire, 23 cm (9 in) long and 0.5 mm (1/16 in) in diameter (thicker wire is difficult to work with).
Green florist's tape
1 piece of stick cinnamon
3 whole cloves
2 pieces of whole ginger

Finely-ground herbs and spices. Use a mixture of the following:
ground cloves
mixed spice
ground nutmeg
ground cinnamon
dried mint
dried rosemary
mixed herbs
aniseed
dried lavender leaves and flowers
1 doily
3 pieces of florist's ribbon for making bows. The colour should match the fabric – approximately 60 cm (24 in) long and 2 mm (1/8 in) wide
1 piece of florist's ribbon in the same colour as those above – approximately 20 cm (8 in) long and 2 mm (1/8 in) wide to tie around the bag
Approximately 25 starflowers in a colour that matches the balls
Clear glue
Essential oil in your favourite aroma
Cotton wool balls – 1 ball per piece of fabric for the large balls and half a ball per piece of fabric for the smaller balls
1 small plastic sandwich bag
A pair of pliers

Method

1. Cut the cinnamon stick in half.
2. Twist a piece of wire around each piece of cinnamon stick and each piece of whole ginger.
3. Divide the starflowers in three bunches by wrapping

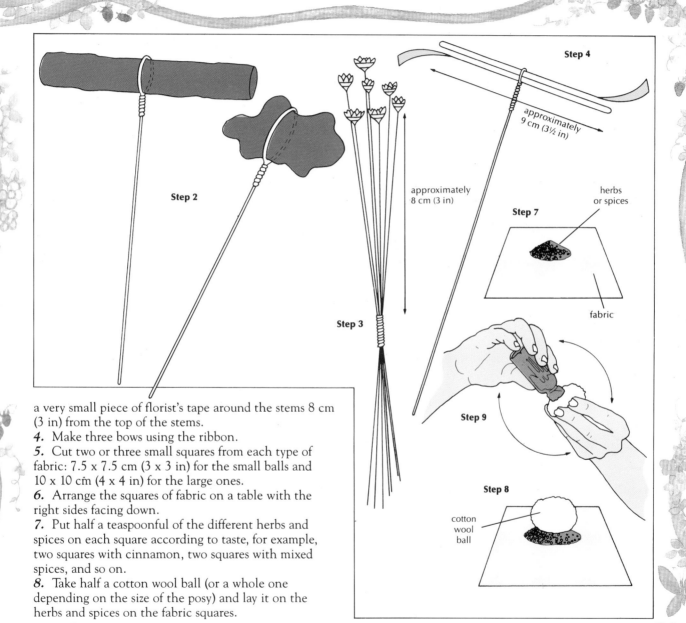

Step 2

approximately 8 cm (3 in)

Step 3

Step 4

approximately 9 cm (3½ in)

herbs or spices

Step 7

fabric

Step 9

Step 8

cotton wool ball

a very small piece of florist's tape around the stems 8 cm (3 in) from the top of the stems.

4. Make three bows using the ribbon.

5. Cut two or three small squares from each type of fabric: 7.5 x 7.5 cm (3 x 3 in) for the small balls and 10 x 10 cm (4 x 4 in) for the large ones.

6. Arrange the squares of fabric on a table with the right sides facing down.

7. Put half a teaspoonful of the different herbs and spices on each square according to taste, for example, two squares with cinnamon, two squares with mixed spices, and so on.

8. Take half a cotton wool ball (or a whole one depending on the size of the posy) and lay it on the herbs and spices on the fabric squares.

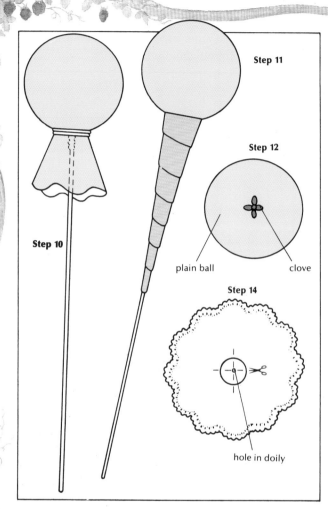

Step 11

Step 12

plain ball   clove

Step 10

Step 14

hole in doily

11. Tie florist's tape around the ends of the fabric square and piece of wire to give it a neat finish. It's unnecessary to cover the entire piece of wire — 7 cm (3 in) from the ball is enough, as part of the wire is snipped off at the end.

12. Take the plain balls and, using a sharp-pointed pair of scissors, cut a tiny hole in the fabric right in the top and middle of the balls. Make a hole in the cotton wool. Cut the stem of a clove to about 4 mm (¼ in), apply some clear glue, and press the clove into the hole.

13. Arrange all the different balls, cinnamon, ginger and flowers together in an attractive round bunch.

14. Insert the stem of this bunch through the hole in the doily and re-arrange the balls until you're satisfied. Sometimes it might be necessary to make the hole in the doily slightly larger by cutting a cross over the hole using a pair of scissors.

15. Wrap all the wires and stems together firmly with florist's tape approximately 4 cm (1½ in) above the doily as well as below it. Do not break the tape; cut the wires and stems to the required length with a small pair of pliers (do not use your scissors!).

16. Cover the rest of the stem and finish the end off.

17. Put the posy in a small plastic bag and firmly secure the bag around the stem with a piece of ribbon. Curl the ends of the ribbon by drawing the blade of a pair of scissors across it. The bag keeps the scent fresh in an attractive package until the recipient opens the gift.

> **HINTS**
> ☐ When flowers are scarce, these posies can be used as table decorations or even as decoration for the aisle at a church wedding. Just imagine the heavenly smell!
> ☐ Keep all the materials for these posies in a large tin. When you suddenly need to make a gift, you'll have everything handy to make one of these posies. You'll even be able to finish one before breakfast!

9. Put a drop of essential oil on three or four of the cotton wool balls and try to cover the spot, or the oil may leave grease marks on the fabric. You can also put oil on each of the cotton wool balls, but this can become quite an expensive exercise.

10. Bring the raw edges of each square together around the cotton wool ball and tie together with wire.

Beeswax candles

These magnificent candles are made from the sheets of wax that beekeepers use to stock the hives. The candles impart a wonderful aroma while burning and are incredibly easy to make; even primary school children manage to make them without any difficulty. They are therefore the perfect gift for teacher or grandma. The wax is available from craft supply stores.

Requirements
1 sheet of beeswax
A piece of string for the wick
Melted candle wax
A craft knife and ruler
Dried flowers
Florist's ribbon
Tape

Method
1. Melt a piece of an ordinary white candle in an empty tincan on the stove. Do not use a saucepan as it is difficult to clean afterwards.
2. Cut the string into three equal lengths, approximately 10 cm (4 in) longer than the candle. Plait the three bits of string into an ordinary plait by knotting the three lengths of string at the one end, plaiting the plait and making a knot at the other end to prevent the plait from coming undone. A single piece of string can also be used as a wick, but you will find that the thicker the wick, the larger the flame will be and the quicker the candle will burn down. With a little practice, you will soon know how thick the wick should be to suit your candles.
3. Dip the wick in the melted wax, remove it and leave it to dry.
4. The size of the candles depends on how the sheets of wax are divided. Whatever shape you choose will be pretty – tall and thin, squat and fat, or small and delicate. Cut the sheets into the required sizes using a sharp knife and ruler. The shape can be rectangular, or you can cut the one side slightly shorter than the opposite side to form a spiral.
5. Lay the wick next to the longest vertical side and fold the wax sheet over it so that the knots protrude on either side. Roll up the sheet of wax. The wax will crack at the first fold, but thereafter it will roll up smoothly.
6. Secure a bunch of dried flowers with a pretty ribbon to the candle with a piece of tape. Curl the ribbon by drawing the blade of a pair of scissors across it.

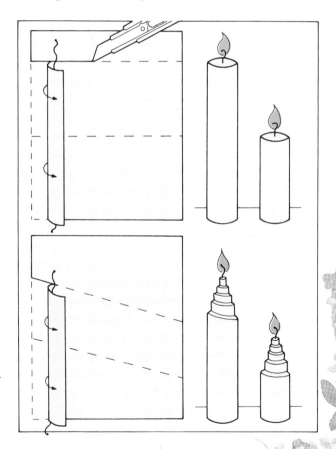

7. Cut the wick flush with the base of the candle and leave about 1 cm (½ in) of the wick at the top. The knots made when the wick was plaited must be cut off during this process.

> ### HINT
> *This is such a pretty gift on its own that it does not need any packaging. Alternatively, you can simply wrap the candle in cellophane. The candles can also be used as Christmas decorations.*

Wedding sampler (see page 56) and beeswax candles.

A straw doll

It's great fun making this straw doll with children. My friend Dana made the very first doll and christened her Kitchen Witch. She supplied the accompanying tale: 'This is a "Kitchen Witch". According to an old Scandinavian legend, a Kitchen Witch prevents the pots from boiling over . . . and stories told in the kitchen from being repeated!' A Kitchen Witch makes a highly original gift.

Requirements
30 pieces of raffia, 62 cm (25 in) long
25 pieces of raffia, 20 cm (8 in) long
Plain cotton fabric for the dress and crown of the cap
Cotton print fabric for the apron and brim of the cap
10 x 12 cm (4 x 5 in) thin bonding fabric
30 cm (12 in) satin ribbon, 13 mm (⅝ in) wide
35 cm (14 in) satin ribbon, 8 mm (⅜ in) wide
16 cm (6½ in) lace for the apron, 1 cm (½ in) wide
A small fabric flower
A few cotton wool balls

Method
1. Gather the long pieces of raffia into a bundle and fold the bundle in half. Firmly tie the bundle 4.5 cm (2 in) from the fold using a separate piece of raffia. Cut the loose ends flush with the knot. This is the doll's head.
2. Gather the short pieces of raffia in a bundle. With one person holding the bundle at one end, another tightly winds the bundle from the other end.
3. Put the ends of the wound-up bundle of raffia on top of each other to make a loop 6 cm (2½ in) long and 3.5 cm (1¼ in) wide. Fasten firmly with a piece of raffia. Cut the loose ends flush with the knot and 2 cm (1 in) from the knot, cut the loose ends of the wound-up bundle evenly. This loop is the doll's arms.
4. Insert half of the loose ends of the larger bundle of raffia through the raffia loop. Move the loop until it is 1.5 cm (¾ in) from the point where the larger bundle is tied together. Tie the larger bundle 4 cm (2 in) from the

first point it was tied. The arms have now been tied.

5. Cut the loose ends of the larger bunch of raffia evenly so that the doll measures 30 cm (12 in).

6. Cut the crown of the cap (pattern on page 87) and a 16 x 25.5 cm (6½ x 10 in) rectangle from the plain fabric.

7. Cut two rectangles from the cotton print fabric, 10 x 12 cm (4 x 5 in) and 14 x 16 cm (5½ x 6½ in) respectively.

8. Make the cap as follows:

Place the bonding fabric on the wrong side of the 10 x 12 cm (4 x 5 in) cotton print rectangle. Fold the piece of fabric and bonding fabric in half lengthwise with the right side facing in. Stitch seams 5 mm (¼ in) wide along the short sides and turn the brim of the cap formed in this way inside out. Mark the centre point of the raw edge.

Stitch the hem along the straight side of the crown as indicated on the pattern on page 87. Gather the crown of the cap as indicated on the pattern, and lay it on the edge of the cap with the right sides, raw edges, ends and centre points even. Stitch the crown and brim

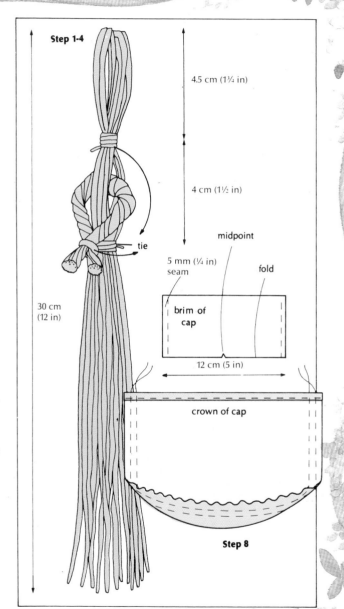

Step 1-4

4.5 cm (1¼ in)

4 cm (1½ in)

tie

midpoint

5 mm (¼ in) seam

fold

brim of cap

12 cm (5 in)

30 cm (12 in)

crown of cap

Step 8

73

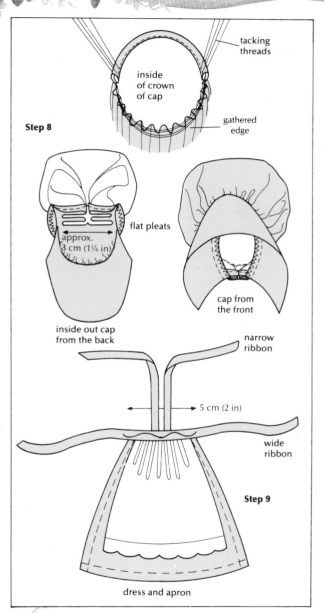

Step 8

inside of crown of cap

tacking threads

gathered edge

flat pleats

approx. 3 cm (1¼ in)

inside out cap from the back

cap from the front

narrow ribbon

5 cm (2 in)

wide ribbon

Step 9

dress and apron

together, allowing 8 mm (⅜ in) for the seam, and carefully zigzag the edge.

Remove the tacking and determine the centre point of the back straight hem of the cap, and make 2½ flat pleats on both sides of this point. Firmly sew together by hand.

Stuff the ball with cotton wool balls and put it on the doll's head. Firmly sew the cap to the doll.

9. Make the dress as follows:

Sew seams along the short sides of the two rectangles. Sew a 1.5 cm (¾ in) seam at the bottom edge of the dress. Sew the lace to the bottom of the apron after zigzagging it. Lay the two rectangles on top of each other with the centre points of the remaining unfinished sides on top of each other. Then gather the dress and apron to a width of 5 cm (2 in) and mark the centre point.

Cut the narrow ribbon in half and place one end of each piece on both sides of the centre and at right angles to the stitching, leaving the long ends free. Place the centre point of the wide ribbon on the centre point of the gathered dress and apron so that the ends of the narrow ribbon are covered. Stitch the ribbon to the apron and dress using wave stitch. Carefully cut the ends of the ribbon at an angle and seal them.

10. Put on the dress by tying the wide ribbon at the back and taking the narrow ribbon over the shoulders and tying it at the back of the neck.

11. Pin or tack the flower through the raffia at the knot in the arms.

12. If you're making the doll for a kitchen, you can hang a pretty card with the 'legendary' tale around her neck.

> **HINT**
> *If you have a pair of pinking shears, you can use them to cut out the dress, apron and straps and simply sew it all together. This way it will be much quicker and cheaper to make the doll.*

How to make paper packages for wrapping gifts

Be original and wrap your gifts in these adorable packages, which you can easily make yourself from bought gift-wrapping.

Flat envelope bags

Use one of these bags for wrapping flat gifts such as framed pictures, a mobile or a round potpourri bag.

Requirements

Gift-wrap paper
A stick of all-purpose glue
A ruler
An air-soluble pen
A pair of scissors

Method

1. Determine the measurements of the gift to be wrapped.
2. Cut the bag from the paper according to the solid lines on the diagram. Use an air-soluble pen to draw lines on the paper — they disappear eventually without leaving a trace.
3. Fold the paper along the dotted lines P and glue A to A.
4. Fold the bag along dotted line Q. Glue B to B, and C to C. The corners of the flap can be cut at an angle before glueing C to C.

Gift-wrapping bags

Use one of these bags to wrap gifts that are an awkward shape, such as covered coat hangers, kitchen witches and jars or bottles. Adjust the sizes according to your needs. You can even make giant bags using two sheets of gift-wrapping.

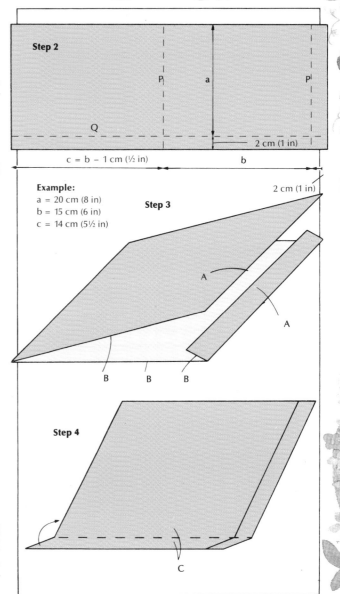

Requirements

Gift-wrap paper
A stick of all-purpose glue
A piece of narrow ribbon or soft, thin string
A ruler
An air-soluble pen
A pair of scissors
A hole punch

Method

1. Determine the measurements of the gift to be wrapped.
2. Cut the bag according to the solid lines on the diagram. Use the air-soluble pen to draw the lines.
3. Fold the paper along the dotted line Q and fold it open again. Then fold on dotted lines P1 and P2 and glue A to A.
4. Fold the bag flat and fold corners S to make fold lines R.
5. To form the base of the bag, fold it as shown, glue D to D, and then E to E. Let glue set.
6. Flatten the bag and punch in two holes at the top of

the opening. A small bag will have eight holes and a large bag four. To prevent the holes from tearing, glue a rectangular piece of cardboard to the inside before punching in the holes.
7. Thread a piece of ribbon or string through the holes and tie a pretty bow to close the bag.

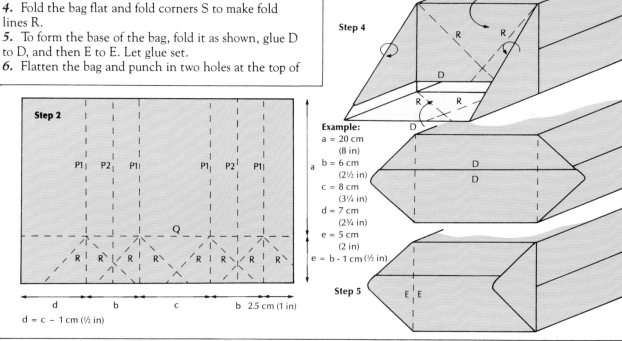

Step 2

Step 3

Step 4

Step 5

Example:
a = 20 cm
(8 in)
b = 6 cm
(2½ in)
c = 8 cm
(3¼ in)
d = 7 cm
(2¾ in)
e = 5 cm
(2 in)
e = b - 1 cm (½ in)

d = c − 1 cm (½ in)

HINT
Cut small hearts from pretty plain, gold or silver paper and use them to seal the envelope bags closed. Use self-adhesive paper that can be removed without damaging the bag when it is opened.

HINTS

□ *A parcel wrapped in plain brown paper can look pretty good if it is decorated with florist's ribbon and a posy of dried or fresh flowers.*

□ *Make a bow from ribbon. It's very easy to make a pretty, professional-looking bow from florist's ribbon to decorate a gift.*

ribbon roll from above

tie with thread   V-shaped notch

1. Roll up 2.25 m (2½ yd) of 2 cm (1 in) wide ribbon and flatten it to a roll 10 cm (4 in) long.

2. Mark the centre, ie a point approximately 5 cm (2 in) from each end.

3. Using a pair of sharp scissors, cut two V-shaped notches opposite each other at the centre point of the ribbon so that the ribbon is approximately 2 mm (⅛ in) wide at that point.

4. Wrap a piece of thread tightly around this narrow section and fasten it tightly.

5. Separate the loops of ribbon with a slightly circular movement to make a pretty bow. Cut the loose ends at an angle with a pair of scissors.

6. The bow can be made even more festive by using two or three colours of ribbon.

7. You can also use wider ribbon, but cut it shorter or the bow will be too bulky.

A balsawood mobile

This balsawood mobile will be appreciated by young and old alike. We've made one using a Christmas theme, but the possibilities are endless. Farm or wild animals, fish, birds, flowers, different kinds of homes or holidays all make excellent themes.

Paint the wood a single colour or two or more colours. Use water-based paint or ordinary diluted food colouring. Either gives the wood an attractive finish. Some food colouring is not water soluble, so take care not to splash it on to clothes or work surfaces.

Requirements

1 embroidery hoop with a diameter of approximately 10 cm (4 in)
1 embroidery hoop with a diameter of approximately 20 cm (8 in)
10 dowels with a diameter of 3 mm (⅛ in) and a length of 8 cm (3 in)
7.5 x 91 cm (3 x 36 in) piece of balsawood, 1.5-3 mm (1/16-⅛ in) thick
A craft knife
A 3-mm (⅛ in) drill bit
Liquid food colouring or water-based paint
Indoor wood sealer (matte finish)
A paintbrush
Thread
Wire wool

Method

1. To make the Christmas mobile, trace the designs from the patterns on the endpapers onto stiff paper or cardboard. Neatly cut out each one and use it as a template.

2. Place the pattern on the balsawood and trace the design onto the wood with a pencil. Retrace the line with the pencil to make a definite groove in the wood. Ensure that any sharp points in the design run parallel with the grain of the wood. Otherwise they have a tendency to snap off.

5. Drill 10 holes through the embroidery hoops using the 3 mm (⅛ in) drill bit. Sand the rings with the wire wool until very smooth.

6. Insert the dowels through the holes in the rings so that the ends of the dowels are flush with the inside of the smaller ring. It's not necessary to glue the dowels as the design is quite stable, and if your measurements are accurate, the dowels should fit snugly.

7. Make a small groove at the top of each dowel, 1 cm (½in) from the outer end by gently pressing the blade of the craft knife into the wood. The threads on which the figures will hang are inserted into these grooves to make them secure.

8. Using a needle, insert thread through each figure at the point from which it is to be hung.

9. Mix the paint or food colouring to the required colour and paint each figure as well as the rings and dowels. Hang them up to dry.

10. Paint a layer of matte wood sealer over the dry paint to get a nice shine.

11. Following the diagram on page 96, mark the three points on the outer ring from which the mobile is hung. Fasten a piece of thread 30 cm (12 in) long around the ring at each of these points. Tie them together around a brass ring from which to hang the mobile.

12. Hang the figures on threads of different lengths from the grooves in the dowels that have been made for this purpose. Adjust them if necessary.

3. Insert the blade of the craft knife into the wood and draw it along the groove forming the design three times. Be very careful, because if you attempt to cut through the wood the first time, it could snap and splinter and look very untidy.

4. Put the inside ring of the two embroidery hoops on the diagram on page 96. Mark the position of the holes for the dowels with a pencil.

HINTS

☐ *Instead of using wooden figures, hang stuffed hearts of contrasting colours (see page 32) from the wooden dowels. If you are using hearts, remember to stuff them with sweet-smelling material before hanging them.*

☐ *An unusual sparkling effect is achieved by dissolving a little gold poster paint in the water used to dilute the paint or food colouring.*

Cotton reel rack

Everyone who does needlework knows how difficult it is to keep cotton reels neatly in order so that they are clearly visible and within easy reach. This nifty rack solves all these problems and is pretty besides.

With a bit of imagination, the basic design of the rack could be adapted slightly to make a handy spice rack to use in the kitchen. Remove one shelf, adjust the spacing and add a narrow strip of wood to the front of each shelf.

Requirements

The following pieces of wood, each 12 mm (½ in) thick:
  2 pieces of 7 x 47 cm (2¾ x 19 in) for the sides
  5 pieces of 8 x 30 cm (3⅛ x 12 in) for the shelves
  1 piece of 10 x 29.5 cm (4 x 11½ in) for the back
55 dowels with a diameter of 3 mm (⅛ in) and a length of
  3.5 cm (1½ in)
28 panel pins, 20 mm (¾ in) long
A pencil
Cold glue
Indoor wood sealer (matte finish)
Sandpaper   *Plastic wood*
Tools as described   *Wood stain*

Method

1. Using a small fretsaw, prepare the different planks for the rack by cutting out the curves as indicated on the sketch and diagram on page 95: the top front corners of the two side planks and two front corners of the five planks for the shelves are each rounded. Cut the plank for the back into a gable shape after drawing the profile on the wood with a pencil.

2. Sand down all the sides and flat surfaces. It is quite difficult to sand the rack once it's assembled.

3. Make five grooves in each of the side planks, 2.5 mm (⅛ in) deep and 12 mm (½ in) wide, with the bottom of each groove 10 cm (4 in) apart. These grooves can be made with a chisel, but experienced woodworkers may want to use an electric radial saw.

4. Prepare the dowels by sawing them to the required length and slightly sharpening one end of each dowel (like a pencil) so that they can be inserted into the holes later.

5. Mark the positions of the dowels on each shelf. Drill a hole with a 3-mm (⅛ in) drill bit at each of these points. The holes should be perpendicular to the horizontal surfaces of the shelves and 5 mm (³⁄₁₆ in) deep. An adjustable drill stand is very useful for this purpose.

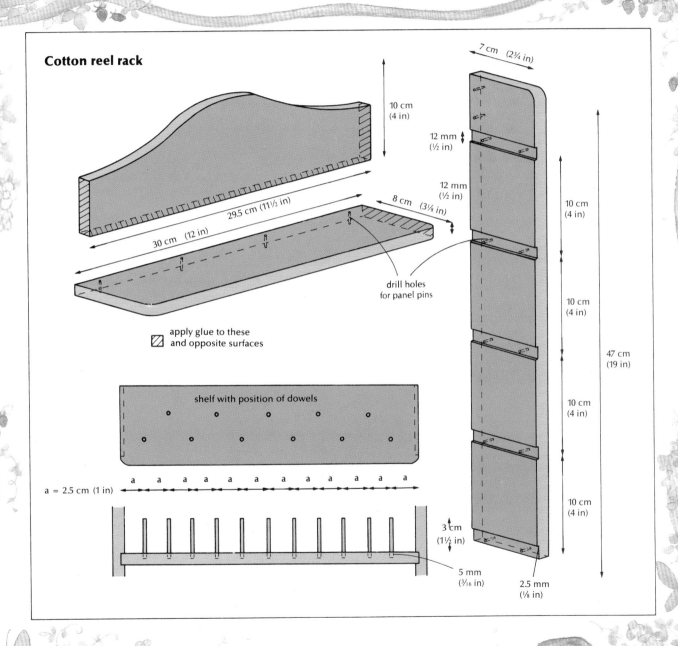

Cotton reel rack

10 cm (4 in)

29.5 cm (11½ in)

30 cm (12 in)

8 cm (3⅛ in)

apply glue to these and opposite surfaces

drill holes for panel pins

7 cm (2¾ in)

12 mm (½ in)

12 mm (½ in)

10 cm (4 in)

10 cm (4 in)

47 cm (19 in)

10 cm (4 in)

10 cm (4 in)

shelf with position of dowels

a = 2.5 cm (1 in)

a a a a a a a a a a a a

3 cm (1½ in)

5 mm (³⁄₁₆ in)

2.5 mm (⅛ in)

6. The rack can now be assembled. With a pencil, mark all the positions where the panel pins have to be hammered in. Using a small drill bit, drill a hole through the upper one of the two planks that are to be secured together. This will prevent the wood from splitting when you hammer in the panel pins.

7. Apply a cold glue to the parts of the rack that are to be assembled and hammer in the panel pins. Sink in their heads so that the holes that are formed can be filled with plastic wood. Put the rack in a clamp and leave for at least two hours to dry. Note that the dowels have not yet been inserted.

8. Fill the holes formed by the panel pins with plastic wood and leave to dry thoroughly.

9. Using fine sandpaper, sand the rack again to remove any sharp edges and rough spots.

10. If you wish to colour the rack, apply the stain at this stage, using a piece of lint-free cloth. Remember to stain the wooden dowels as well. Allow the stain to dry.

11. Firmly hammer the wooden dowels into the holes. If you have worked accurately, it won't be necessary to glue them as they will fit snugly.

12. Add the final finish to the rack by coating it with wood sealer. Two layers are generally required for a smooth, even matte finish.

13. The rack can stand on its own on a table or in a cupboard. An even better idea is to hang it up on a hook against a wall.

> **HINTS**
> ☐ *Any attractive wood can be used for the rack. Because pine is commonly available and stains well, it has been used in the illustrations.*
> ☐ *Do not drop glue on the surfaces you wish to stain, as the glue will seal the wood and prevent the stain from penetrating it.*
> ☐ *Remember always to test the stain first on a wood off-cut before applying it to the item you're making.*

Candle holder

This type of wall rack was used for storing candles in the days before electricity. Today it is purely decorative or can be used as a holder for ornaments or a small vase of flowers. It's perfect for a large beeswax candle and makes a very original gift.

Requirements
The following pieces of wood, each 12 mm (½ in) thick:
    1 piece 14.5 x 40 cm (5¾ x 15¾ in) for the back
    2 pieces 9.5 x 27 cm (3¾ x 10½ in) for the sides
    1 piece 9.5 x 12 cm (3¾ x 4¾ in) for the shelf
Cold glue
13 panel pins, 20 mm (¾ in) long
Plastic wood
Wood stain
Indoor wood sealer (matte finish)
Sandpaper
Tools as described

Method
1. Prepare the separate panels for the rack by cutting out the curves and patterns with a fretsaw as indicated on the sketch and diagrams on page 95. Use a large drill bit to make the hole in the back.

2. Sand all the sides and flat surfaces of the pieces of wood before assembling the rack.

3. Using a pencil, mark all the positions where the panel pins have to be hammered in. Using a small drill bit, drill a hole through the upper of the two planks that are to be secured together. This will prevent the wood from splitting when you hammer in the panel pins.

4. Carefully apply a little cold glue to the parts of the rack that are to be assembled and then hammer in the panel pins. Sink in their heads so that the holes that are formed can be filled with plastic wood. Put the rack firmly in a clamp and leave for at least two hours to dry.

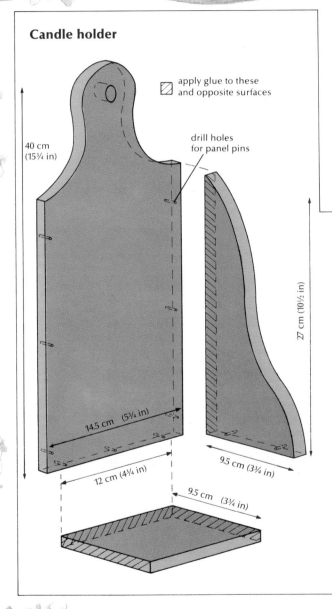

Candle holder

40 cm
(15¾ in)

apply glue to these
and opposite surfaces

drill holes
for panel pins

27 cm (10½ in)

14.5 cm (5¾ in)

9.5 cm (3¾ in)

12 cm (4¾ in)

9.5 cm   (3¾ in)

5. Fill the holes formed by the panel pins with plastic wood and leave to dry thoroughly.

6. Using fine sandpaper, sand the rack again to remove any sharp edges and rough spots.

7. If you intend staining the wood, apply the stain with a lint-free cloth. Leave the stain to dry thoroughly.

8. Add the final finish to the rack by coating it with wood sealer. Two layers are generally required for an even matte finish.

Letter and key rack

This letter and key rack will keep your keys and mail in a safe and handy place.

Requirements

The following pieces of wood, each 12 mm (½ in) thick:
  1 piece 14.5 x 28 cm (5¾ x 11 in) for the back
  1 piece 9.5 x 14.5 cm (3¾ x 5¾ in) for the front
  1 piece 9.5 x 14.5 cm (3¾ x 5¾ in) for the bottom
  2 pieces 9.5 x 11 cm (3¾ x 4⅜ in) for the sides
Cold glue
18 panel pins, 20 mm (¾ in) long
Plastic wood
Wood stain
Indoor wood sealer (matte finish)
Sandpaper
5 brass hooks

Method

1. Follow the instructions for the candle holder.
2. If you are using the rack for keeping keys, insert the hooks at the bottom of the rack 3.8 cm (1½ in) apart and 4.75 cm (1⅞ in) from the back (not shown).

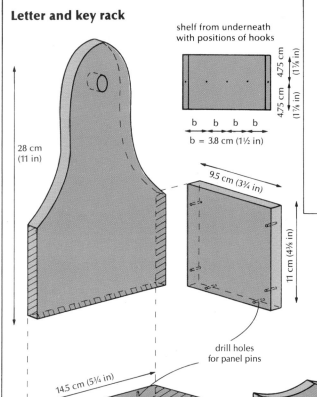

Letter and key rack

shelf from underneath with positions of hooks

4.75 cm (1⅞ in)
4.75 cm (1⅞ in)

b   b   b   b
b = 3.8 cm (1½ in)

28 cm (11 in)

9.5 cm (3¾ in)

11 cm (4⅜ in)

drill holes for panel pins

14.5 cm (5¾ in)

9.5 cm (3¾ in)

14.5 cm (5¾ in)

9.5 cm (3¾ in)

apply glue to these and opposite surfaces

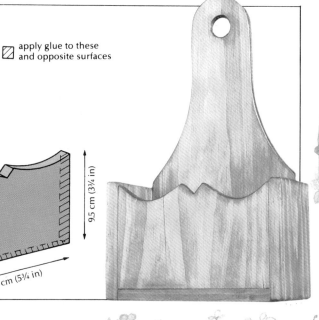

Project index

HEARTS AND DOVES FOR A LITTLE GIRL
(see page 47)
PATTERN, ACTUAL SIZE

A STRAW DOLL
(see page 72)
PATTERN, ACTUAL SIZE

Crown of cap

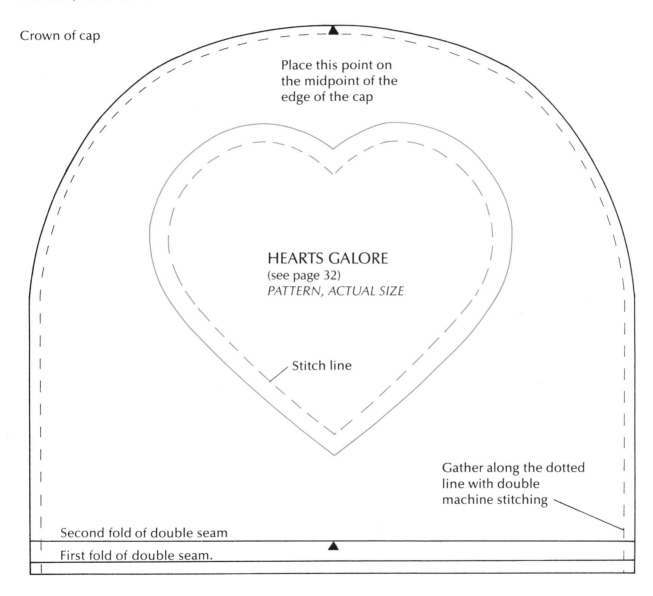

Place this point on
the midpoint of the
edge of the cap

HEARTS GALORE
(see page 32)
PATTERN, ACTUAL SIZE

Stitch line

Gather along the dotted
line with double
machine stitching

Second fold of double seam

First fold of double seam.

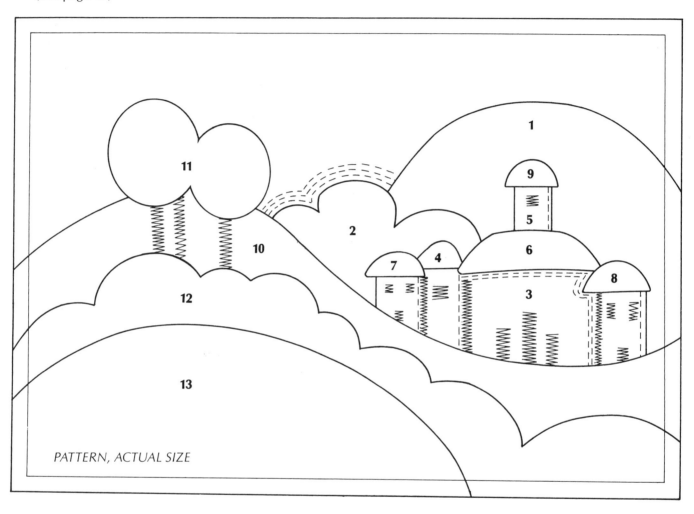

PATTERN, ACTUAL SIZE

$\lessgtr$ and – – – – are machine stitches added afterwards

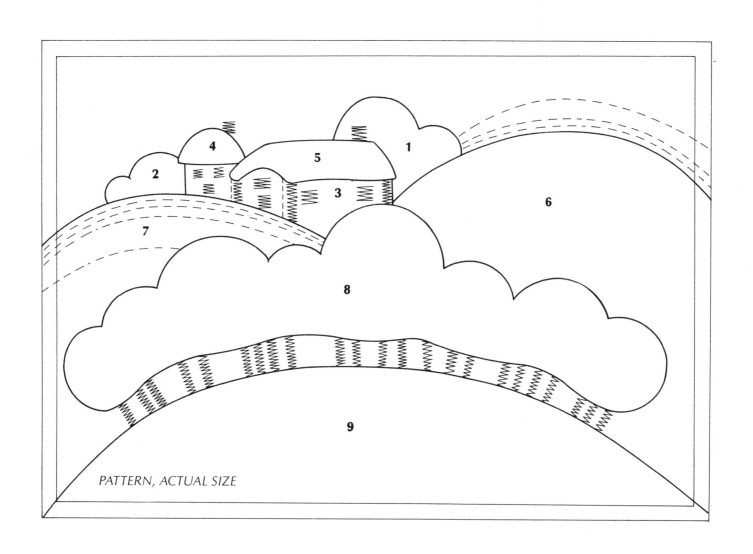

PATTERN, ACTUAL SIZE

〰 and ― ― ― ― are machine stitches added afterwards

HEARTS IN CROSSES

Symbol	DMC	Colour
•	3042	Light antique violet
▫	3041	Dark antique violet
✚	327	Violet

BACKSTITCHES

		Gold thread
——		

CHEFS FOR THE KITCHEN

Symbol	DMC	Colour
<	817	Red
✚	000	White
•	898	Dark brown
+	437	Light brown
✕	727	Light yellow
▫	445	Bright yellow
▼	741	Orange
✕	820	Dark blue
○	799	Light blue
\	700	Green
▿	712	Flesh colour
■	754	Pink

BACKSTITCHES

—	898	Dark brown
	817	Red

HOME SWEET HOME

Symbol	DMC	Colour
✚	000	White
◆	221	Dark shell pink
^	645	Very dark beaver grey
▫	647	Medium beaver grey
▿	677	Very light old gold
:	729	Medium old gold
/	781	Dark topaz
\	924	Very dark grey-green
-	926	Dark grey-green
+	927	Medium grey-green
✕	935	Dark avocado green
✹	3031	Very dark mocha brown
○	3041	Medium antique violet
⁞	3042	Light antique violet
◀	3051	Dark grey-green
<	3052	Medium grey-green

BACKSTITCHES

——	221	Border frame
	924	Lattice-work on roof; top edge of gable
	3031	All other; personal details
	781	Bird's eyes

FRENCH KNOTS

•	924	House
	3031	Doorknob, birds' eyes
	729	Roof

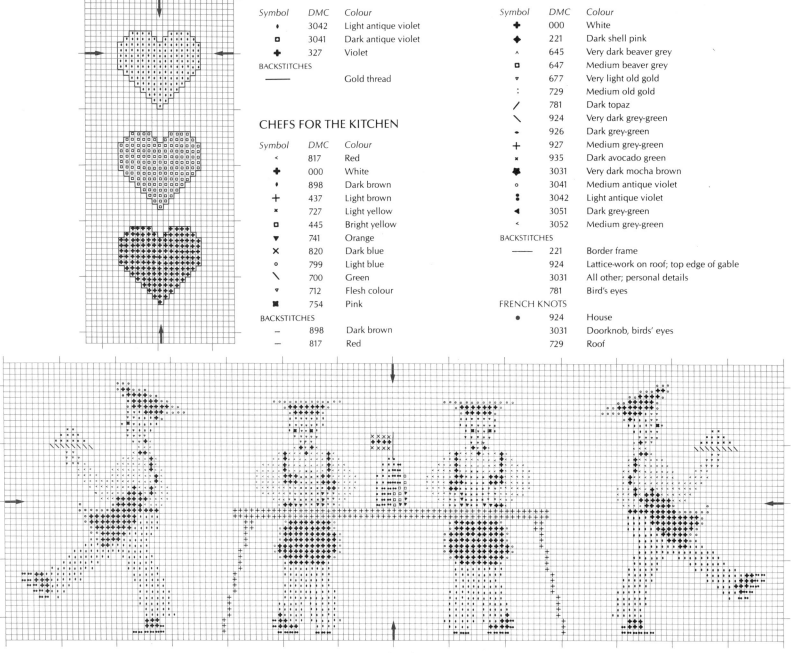

SINGING QUARTET

Symbol	DMC	Colour
◇	975	Dark golden brown
<	433	Medium brown
^	437	Light tan
+	754	Light peach flesh
:	353	Peach flesh
>	3064	Medium sportsman flesh
♠	367	Dark pistachio green
/	320	Medium pistachio green
⁞	368	Light pistachio green
▽	304	Medium Christmas red
··	415	Pearl grey
▢	317	Pewter grey
\	926	Dark grey-green
▶	927	Medium grey-green
✖	924	Very dark grey-green
✕	680	Dark old gold
–	930	Dark antique blue
○	3047	Light yellow beige
∨	746	Off-white
✿	729	Medium old gold
▨	3371	Black-brown
×	840	Medium beige-brown
✚	842	Light beige-brown
••	838	Dark beige-brown

BACKSTITCHES

	DMC	Colour
～～～	729	Light rays
────	801	All other

WEDDING SAMPLER

Symbol	DMC	Colour
⬟	738	Flesh
✕	310	Black
+	727	Light yellow
••	444	Bright yellow
▼	963	Light pink
▢	603	Pink
\	600	Dark pink
✚	699	Grass green
▾	435	Light brown
▨	801	Dark brown
•	798	Blue
✕	820	Cobalt blue

BACKSTITCHES———

The same as nearest cross stitch except
eyes (820) and butterflies near tree (435).
Fill in initials between the hearts at the top
(738), and wedding date (820) lower down.

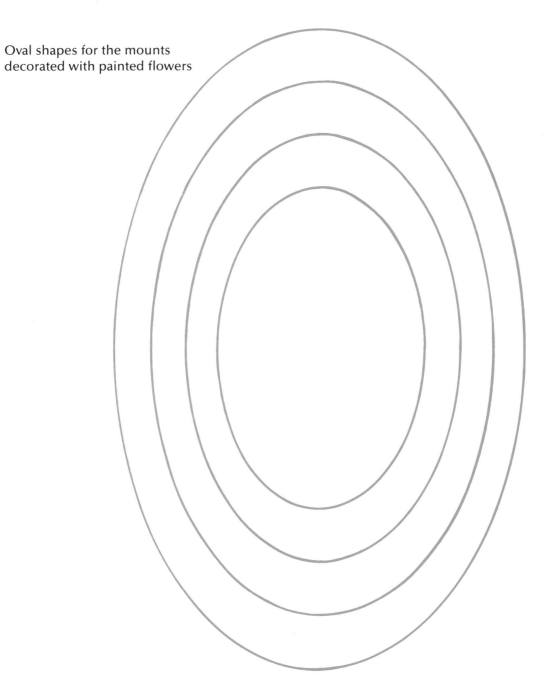

Oval shapes for the mounts
decorated with painted flowers

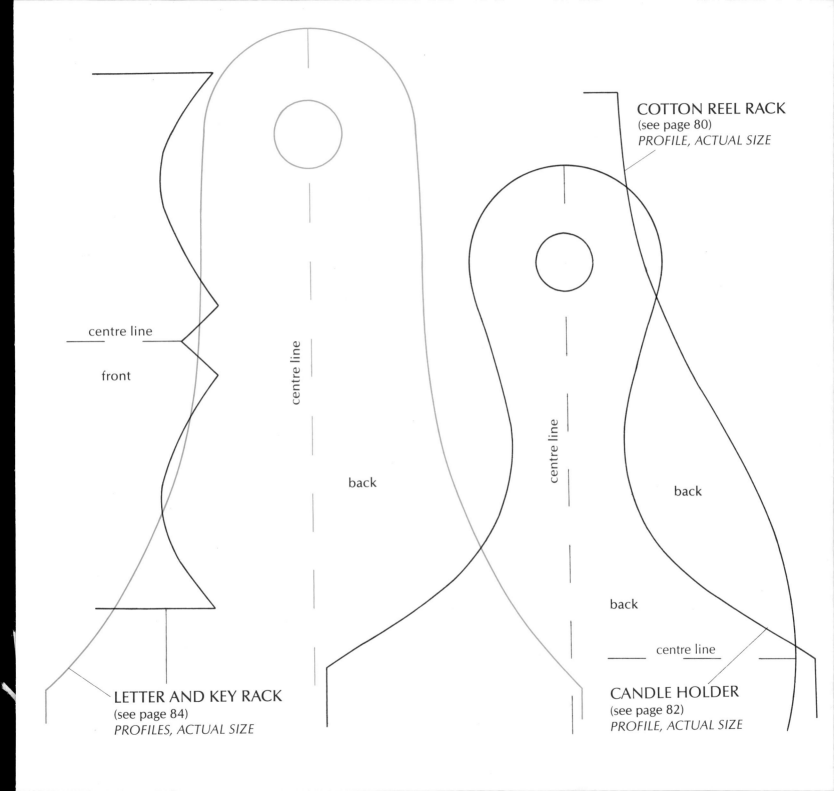

centre line

front

centre line

LETTER AND KEY RACK
(see page 84)
PROFILES, ACTUAL SIZE

centre line

back

centre line

back

back

centre line

COTTON REEL RACK
(see page 80)
PROFILE, ACTUAL SIZE

CANDLE HOLDER
(see page 82)
PROFILE, ACTUAL SIZE

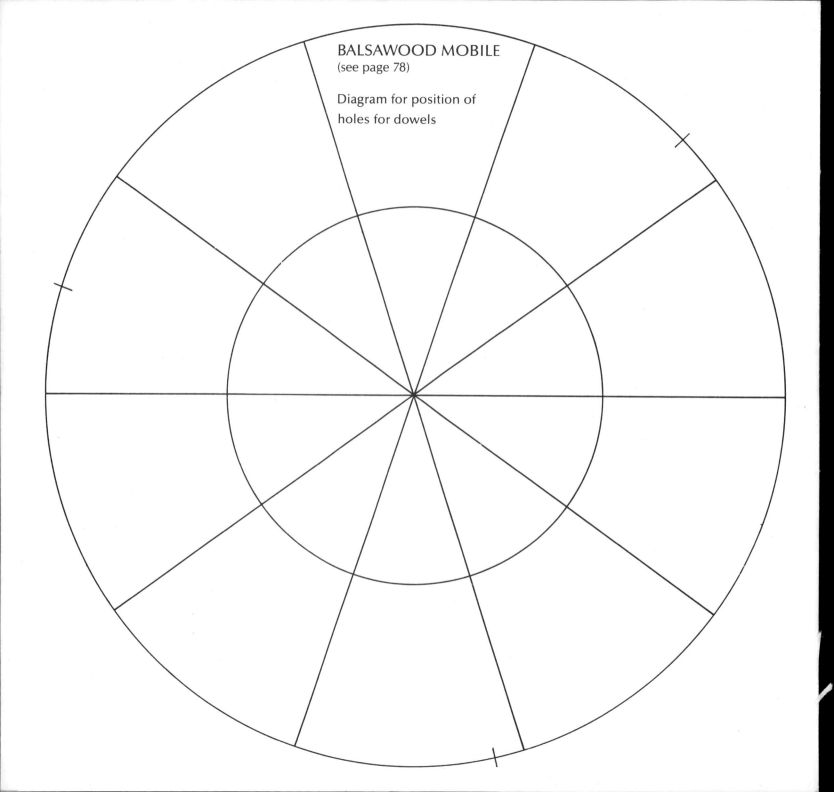

BALSAWOOD MOBILE
(see page 78)

Diagram for position of
holes for dowels